Lennart Johansson

A Mate Among Bigwigs and Trophies
AIK, UEFA, FIFA and Beyond

Lennart Johansson
Sören 'Sulo' Karlsson

NEW HAVEN PUBLISHING LTD

Published 2025
First Edition
New Haven Publishing Ltd
www.newhavenpublishingltd.com
newhavenpublishing@gmail.com

All Rights Reserved
The rights of Lennart Johansson and Sören 'Sulo' Karlsson, as the authors of this work, have been asserted in accordance with the Copyrights, Designs and Patents Act 1988.
No part of this book may be re-printed or reproduced or utilized in any form or by any electronic, mechanical or other means, now unknown or hereafter invented, including photocopying, and recording, or in any information storage or retrieval system, without the written permission of the Authors and Publisher.

Cover design©Pete Cunliffe
Lennart Johansson private image gallery©Lennart family by Benny Jansson

Copyright © 2025 Lennart Johansson &
Sören 'Sulo' Karlsson
All rights reserved
ISBN: 978-1-915975-10-2

For Eva, Benny and Lena

Thank you to Stefan Jonasson

Content

Foreword My Friend 'Musse'		9
Lennart Johansson Career		14
Prologue		15
1	A Working Class Boy Watches his First Football Match at Råsunda	18
2	Hitler and Jesse Owens	25
3	War and Love	29
4	AIK Relegated; But Happiness in my Private Life	36
5	Family, Advancement and a New Friendship	40
6	Unforgettable Goals and Political Quarrels	46
7	Stepping Up	50
8	Knocked Out by Ingo and a Dear Reunion	53
9	The Start of My Career in the Top Job at AIK	58
10	The Greatest Football Player Retires	61
11	Total Football and an Approaching Disaster	64
12	Storms on All Fronts	68
13	Football and Politics	73
14	Sweden in the Football Elite	77

| 15 | Alcohol Shows No Mercy | 81 |

Gallery of Lennarts Private images

16	An Uncorrupted Role Model and a Scandal	86
17	As One Star Dies, Another is Born	90
18	The Step up to the Top	96
19	The Shot	100
20	The Tournament of Champions	106
21	Success and Falling Stars	111
22	Into the Lion's Den	118
23	Catching My Breath at Vätö	122
24	Money Money Money	125
25	Death's Group and Death's Grip	129
26	Me and the Media	133
27	Blatter Gets Booed and AIK in Crisis	136
28	A Message of Sorrow and a Last Attempt	141
29	A Match Within the Match	145
30	The Long Road Out of Defeat	152
31	Life's Brutality and a Beautiful Victory	156

Epilogue The Dirty Game	161
Postscript	163
About the Author with Lennart Johansson	171

"It is, on Thursday, twenty-seven thousand six hundred and twelve days since the day I saw the premiere at Råsunda in 1937. Or closer to two billion four hundred million seconds ago. I was seven years old then. Today I am eighty-three. But at the same time, it is difficult to understand the passage of time and a journey that corresponds to almost one's entire life through these numbers that form large, abstract numbers.

It is only the memories that can weave the story together and make it comprehensible."

- From Lennart Johansson's farewell speech to the Råsunda football stadium on November 21, 2012

Foreword

My Friend 'Musse'

"Do you know what the best thing about this book is?" asked Lennart suddenly, during one of the many interviews I did with him for this book about his life.

"No," I answered.

"The best thing about this book is that we have met, talked and become friends," said Lennart, and suddenly I saw something intense and curious in his eyes that I had not noticed before.

Of course, I was moved by his words, and even though we had come a long way into the work, the continuation somehow became both simpler and more profound. We were friends - buddies, and if you are buddies, you can talk about anything without it feeling artificial. At the same time, I learned that Lennart was not called anything other than 'Musse' by his close friends and therefore I would also say 'Musse' from now on.

Lennart often said that his career in world football was actually mostly due to chance. That he was in the right place at the right time and pretty much always accepted various board assignments and positions he was offered. Perhaps the same can be said about why I was asked to write his life story.

Although for some time I have become something of an AIK (Swedish football club) figure through my work leading conferences at Hovet in connection with the hockey matches, and through the book I wrote about the AIK twins Yngve and Börje Leback, the assignment came rather unexpectedly.

I got a call from Stefan Jonasson, commercial manager at AIK Football, who wanted us to have a meeting. When Stefan then told me that it was about the opportunity to write Lennart Johansson's biography, it felt almost surreal.

"Can you imagine doing that?" Stefan asked, and I answered "yes" even though I obviously hadn't had time to think through what such an honourable mission would entail.

"When do you want it to be ready?" I wondered.

"What about when AIK wins the gold cup this autumn and Lennart's trophy comes home?" answered Stefan.

I laughed because this was in May 2018 and it meant that I would have to write the book in six months. When no one else laughed, I understood that it was a serious wish.

"Ok," I said, and then Stefan called Lennart, who thought the arrangement sounded like a good idea. We decided we would meet in connection with the next home game and then the work would be started as soon as possible.

Perhaps Stefan noticed that I looked a little shocked when everything was decided, but he assured me that I was the right man for the job.

"Lennart is a straightforward, honest man with a big heart, so always be straight with him, otherwise he can have a hot temper," said Stefan.

Stefan was right about everything except the temper, and how long it takes to write a book. From the first time Lennart and I met, it became clear that we agreed very much on most things. The work on the book quickly became something other than just work. Of course, there was a lot of interviewing and a lot of writing, as Sweden went through its hottest summer in modern times.

But above all, the friendship became a bridge that blurred the age difference between us and made us talk like friends do about everything and nothing. Although football was our biggest topic of conversation and common denominator, the conversation often drifted into other things.

However, I never saw the hot temper that Stefan warned me about. When I told Lennart about Stefan's warning, he smiled and said, "I have never had a reason to be angry with you."

We also started hanging out outside the book work, and we went to hockey and football matches together. An event that will linger in my memory was when I was visiting Lennart just before Christmas. We had one long conversation, listened to Frank Sinatra and talked about his great interest in music.

In the evening, Lennart was to attend the AIK Ring's annual Christmas dinner. The AIK Ring, which was formed in 1938, is an association for old players and leaders who worked for and meant a lot to the club.

When I was leaving, Lennart asked what I was going to do in the evening.

"I'm thinking about whether I should watch the basketball match between AIK and Hammarby in Solnahallen," I said, to which Lennart replied, "Yes, I want to do that too."

About an hour later, as I had started to write, Mija Lindberg from the football association called and said that she had heard that Lennart and I were going to the basketball match together, and she told me that a car would pick us up and the tickets were in the box office. And, just like that, we are sitting in Solnahallen eating hotdogs.

In some ways, this story paints a picture of Lennart that probably says more about his personality than all the assignments and awards that adorned his career.

I saw, during our time together, that Lennart had succeeded in something that few have been blessed with. He had managed to still be the 'little boy from Åkeshov' who was curious about football, music and all the other good things in life. Despite large and responsible assignments, it was his boyish curiosity that drove him on.

We talked about it a lot - to never look back or let adversity hold you back - and I understood that Lennart had succeeded in living by that motto throughout his life.

After the basic work on the book was finished, we continued to see each other every week, mostly because we both thought it was nice and rewarding to talk about everything between heaven and earth. If we didn't see each other, we talked on the phone, and we planned for Lennart's

90th birthday and the book release, which had been postponed and was now planned for the autumn of 2019. Since I turned 50 that year, we said we would celebrate our 140th together. It didn't turn out that way. Lennart's big heart, which beat for his daughters, wives, AIK and football at all its levels, couldn't make it all the way.

Even if he felt a little weak towards the end, there was no way he wouldn't fly to Baku as UEFA's honorary president and see the Europa League final.

Despite the fact that several people close to him thought he should stay at home, he stuck to his decision.

"I'm not going to stay at home. If my time on this earth is over then I want to fall at my post," said Lennart and flew to Baku.

It was planned that after Baku he would fly directly to Madrid where the Champions League final, the cup he himself created, would take place. But Lennart, despite his stubbornness and devotion, had to change his plans.

He flew home. Home to Stockholm and the apartment at Stora Essingen. Then everything happened very quickly, at least for those of us who were on the sidelines. On Friday, he suffered a cardiac arrest at home and was taken by ambulance to St. Göran's hospital.

I visited Lennart on Saturday, the same day that the Champions League final between Liverpool and Tottenham was played. I was alone but I talked about everything and nothing as usual and the doctor thought there was a possibility that Lennart could actually hear me. I called him Musse so he would know there was a friend there.

The next day, AIK played a derby against Hammarby and I didn't know if I would be able to go because Lennart was so bad. But I decided that, of course, he would have wanted me to. It was a particularly emotional match for me as AIK won with a clear 2-0 after the best effort of the season so far.

Afterwards, Stefan Jonasson and I went up to Lennart with the match ball, signed by all the AIK players. Lennart also got my AIK scarf and we talked about today's victory, although we didn't know if he heard us. Then there was a few days of waiting for the inevitable end. Since I had spent the last year writing down Lennart's life story, it was hard not to look back and reflect.

I thought of the little boy from Åkeshov who cycled into Råsunda to see his beloved AIK. Musse, who together with his mates used to stand outside the entrance and ask if any kind adult could help them in. It always ended with someone lifting him over the turnstile so he didn't have to pay, and once inside he ran to the billboard behind 'Gurra' Sjöberg's goal.

Late in the evening on June 4th, 2019, Lennart's heart stopped beating. Lennart 'Musse' Johansson was back at the entrance and was lifted over the turnstile for the last time.

Thank you, Musse, for your friendship, all the fruitful conversations, incredible stories and all your care and wisdom. If it's possible to be larger than life, you are. Although you are no longer with us, your life's work lives on forever.

Your Friend
Sören 'Sulo' Karlsson

Lennart Johansson Career

1937 Watches his first match at Råsunda
1941 Founds IK Hjelm
1961 Chairman of the bandy section in AIK
1962 Chairman of the AIK football board
1967 Chairman of the main board of AIK
1978 Chairman of Swedish Elite Football, SEF
Supervisor for the Swedish World Cup delegation in Argentina
1984 Board member of Tipstjänst (Swedish pools betting)
1985 Chairman of the Swedish Football Association
1990 Takes office as president of UEFA
1992 Creates the Champions League
1994 Supreme manager of the World Cup in the USA
1998 Candidate for the presidency of FIFA
Top manager of World Cup in France
1999 Honorary chairman of AIK
2001 The Swedish league cup is renamed 'Lennart Johansson's Trophy'
2002 Supreme manager of the World Cup in Japan/South Korea
2006 Supreme manager of the World Cup in Germany
2007 Resigns as UEFA president and is appointed honorary chairman
2007 Elected to Swedish football's Hall of Fame
2012 Watches the last match at Råsunda
2016 Founds the Lennart Johansson Foundation

Prologue

Stockholm 2019

It's lonely here without her, I think. I walk around the apartment on Stora Essingen and look out over Essinge cove and the waters of Mälaren. It's been almost ninety years. It sounds incredible when I think about it. On the other side of the water I see Äppel cove. When I turn around after a while and look towards the bookshelf, my eyes are fixed on a picture.

Lennart with HRH Queen Elisabeth II

I was the president of UEFA, and it was the European Championship in England in 1996. The greatness of the moment was felt in my body. I was like in a fog. It's hard to describe the feeling of standing in the middle of a packed football stadium; everywhere you look it's full of people. You can feel the collective energy as a gigantic force. Frustrated, like a chained, hungry dragon. The sound is also hard to describe, but when I close my eyes I hear it clearly. I feel the power. I was responsible for escorting Queen Elizabeth II and introducing all the English players to her before the semi-final against Germany. The Queen of England. I? The little boy from Åkeshov? There was only three years age difference between me and Queen Elisabeth II, but there I was, in awe like a little boy. When she looked at me it was like she was looking at a little boy with sore knees and cap in hand. Although I was quite good at English, I struggled to understand her aristocratic pronunciation and choice of words.

When we got down on the pitch, all the players were introduced to her and every time someone said their name the Queen would ask, "How do you spell it?" whereupon each player had to spell his name as clearly as possible while the rumbling sound from the stands of a packed Wembley roared around us.

It was after this that I did the unforgivable. We made our way up to the VIP seats, which were reserved for royalty, high-ranking politicians, selected rock stars, actresses and other high-profile celebrities. I obviously didn't know at the time, but it is strictly forbidden to walk behind a female royal up a flight of stairs. But that's exactly what I did. A muffled voice came obliquely from behind me, from a stressed out FIFA employee who pointed out my blatant mistake. I quickly got up next to her, but by then it was already too late.

The Queen's gaze cut through the noise and clearly showed, with all the weight of her office, that I should know my place and that I had done wrong.

We chatted a bit. The Queen asked me, among other things, about the weather in Sweden, and since it was just over a week after midsummer, I replied that it was probably as warm and sunny as here in England. I felt troubled by the situation. There was something I didn't like about her way of talking, the way she looked at me and others around us.

She was very nice and spread polite phrases around her, but I still didn't feel quite comfortable in her company.

After the match, neither the Queen of England nor her people were particularly pleased. I can still see her stony face in front of me. The semi-final was lost against England's arch-rival Germany. To top it all it was lost on penalties, just like against Germany in the World Cup semi-final in 1990. It was different in 1966, when England won their only World Cup title to date by defeating the Germans at Wembley – with the Queen in the stands – after a dramatic extra time with two goals by Geoff Hurst.

Now there was also extra time, but without a goal being scored. And a penalty shootout is not England's best talent. All of them took their penalties right up to the very last one, which was to be taken by Aston Villa centre-back Gareth Southgate. It was an effort that would put a dark mark on Southgate's life for a long time, a poorly struck penalty that Germany's keeper had no problem catching. It was completely quiet at Wembley, waiting for Germany's last penalty taker, Andreas Möller, to shoot. The silence was as tangible and concrete as the cheering afterwards. Of course he put it right in the goal. The Germans' ability to win on penalties is impressive. They went on to win the European Cup after a final victory against the surprise Czech Republic.

The memories are many. All these meetings, all these people. And I will always be that little boy who thinks: 'Now Dad would probably be proud.'

1

A Working Class Boy Watches his First Football Match at Råsunda

Råsunda old Stadium 1937

My values and my view of society were probably already formed while growing up in Åkeshov outside Stockholm. It was a time when virtues such as community, cooperation and diligence were put first. They were the ideals that permeated everything. People gathered in associations and actively participated in the society that was built so that everyone could belong.

My father, Hilmer Johansson, was a carpenter, and my mother Maria, or Mia as she was called, was a housewife like many women at the time. I was the youngest with four older siblings. Since my siblings were so much older than me, they had to help take care of me, but I also had to learn early to help around the house.

A great role model was my eldest brother Ernst, who was twenty-two years older than me and a police officer.

"Are you going to come along and watch my brother direct the traffic at Tegelbacken?" I used to proudly ask my schoolmates at Olofslund School when I was in the second or third grade.

They stared wide-eyed at the little boy and the big man in a police uniform, with white gloves, who confidently showed the road users when and how they were allowed to drive. Some of them didn't believe me.

"It's not your brother, it's an old man," some of my friends used to say. When I then approached Ernst and he let me into the traffic, they understood that I had indeed spoken the truth. The pride I felt was immense. I also had another brother, Runo, who was twenty-one years older than me and who moved to Gothenburg to work. The fact that my siblings were so much older, with responsible and adult lives, probably shaped the feeling I always carried with me. I had a desire to show myself as a capable person in front of my parents; I didn't want to be the little guy, I wanted to be big and responsible like my siblings.

In addition to my brothers, I had two sisters. Anna was the one who was closest in age to me, but still a full eight years older. My other sister, Gurli, was sixteen years older than me and often took on the role of my extra mother.

The reason for the big age difference between me and my siblings was my father's work, or rather my uncle's work. My uncle had moved to Idaho Falls in the US in the 1920s to seek happiness and employment. After a few years he sent a letter to my father and asked if he could come over and help with the construction of his house.

He also wrote that the Americans were in need of labour and since times were bad in Sweden, Dad went to the US. He must have been in his mid-twenties and he stayed for almost three years. When he came home, I was born nine months later. Dad's stay in the promised land was not quite what he had hoped for. I remember on one occasion I overheard my older brother, Ernst, ask Dad how it was in America.

"There was not much to expect from the Americans. All they do is drink and fight," Dad replied. How he himself had passed the time he did not answer, but he had probably taken the occasional drink himself during his years on the other side of the Atlantic.

Since he had been so disappointed with his time in America, everyone was a bit surprised when he still chose to go there again just a few years after I was born. That time, however, he only stayed for a year. We didn't have much money and Dad drank a little too often, but I got a lot of love. It was a good upbringing.

I was sociable child and made friends easily. Not far from our home was a boarding school called Nockebyhemmet, for boys who for some reason could not live with their parents. Maybe the parents were dead, or they were sick, or drug addicts. I probably never bothered to ask. Some of the boys who lived at the school became my best friends and we had a lot of fun together.

The people who worked there were very careful that the boys were clean and well dressed before they were allowed to come out and play with the rest of us. We all wore shorts as soon as it got warmer than twelve degrees and these were made of some sort of fake material, half cotton and half cellulose, and they were not particularly comfortable. We also wore rough shoes or boots, knee socks, a sweater and a jacket, and the boys from the Nockeby home had to wear a cap regardless of the weather.

Early on I learned that there were kids who were much better off than us ordinary working class children. The growing Bromma area, to which Åkeshov belongs, was close to Drottningholm with Drottningholm's castle, the English park with its sculptures and fountains, and behind the castle the large houses with gardens that stretched right down to the Mälaren waters.

But the children from those families never played with us. I never thought about why that was at the time, it was just an unwritten rule. Later, when I grew up, I came to understand that there were people who chose to separate themselves from certain other people in society.

When I was ten years old, I started working extra and delivering parcels for Konsum (a food store). It was Christmas time at the beginning of the Second World War and many Christmas presents were to be delivered to the luxurious villas behind Drottningholm Palace. There were so many packages that the bike went on its back wheel and I slipped in the sleet and had to fight to keep my balance. Once I arrived and was going to hand the package over to the house or kitchen staff, I had to wait in the hall. If I was lucky, I got a few pennies or sweets as a tip.

At school, children from different backgrounds ended up in the same class and then the differences between us became even clearer. The teacher handed out piggy banks, where we would save a penny every week, and the person who had accumulated the most money at the end of the term received a prize. While my friends and I put in one or two pennies, the rich kids had paper money folded up in their piggy banks. I felt so ashamed when the teacher opened my piggy bank in front of the class. My parents had no money to contribute.

Social differences were very clear at school and in society at large, but there was one place where I felt everyone was equal – it was in sports, and the club I made my own was AIK, Allmänna Idrottsklubben. A club that is for everyone, rich or poor, good or bad, it doesn't matter. The year was 1935 and I was six years old when my brother Runo took me to my first football match. It was before Råsunda was built, so the match was played at Stockholm Stadium. Because I was so small, I didn't have to pay. I will never forget it. An AIK official lifted me over the turnstile so I could enter. Now, in retrospect, I think it was symbolic: I was lifted into the club, welcomed with open arms. That my club became AIK is not surprising because Djurgården was in a division below the highest and

Hammarby was so far down in the divisions that the team was barely on the map. But the geographical location also played a role. If you were born in Bromma or to the north, you became a 'Rat' almost automatically, which was what they called us.

Gustav Sjøberg

My first idol was AIK's goalkeeper Gustav 'Gurra' Sjöberg. He was a fixture in goal until AIK bought Hammarby's star goalkeeper Sven 'Svenne Berka' Bergqvist in the spring of 1936. He wore the goalkeeper shirt in our national team. Many

AIK fans didn't like that Gurra was replaced in the goal because 'Gurra' Sjöberg was the AIK crowd's favourite. Instead of being disappointed, Gurra bit the bullet and fought even harder in training and eventually took his place back, which meant that Svenne Berka had to sit on the bench during the Allsvenskan (the Swedish top league) matches, even though he played in three international matches during that time. He soon returned to Bajen.

It wasn't long before I got to experience my first gold win with AIK - just two years after that match at the Stockholm Stadium. It was 1937 and I was about to turn eight. The season ended in the best possible way. AIK took home the gold with the club's biggest points margin so far, a whopping nine points. Unfortunately, I did not see the gold-winning match because I had contracted measles and was at home in bed. After that, the wait for an SM gold became all the longer - not until 1992 was it time again.

All in all, 1937 was a year that would become imprinted in many Rats' memories. AIK had outgrown the Stockholm Stadium and had to move into the new national arena, Råsunda football stadium. Half the season was played at the Stockholm Stadium, and the team debuted on Råsunda's grass against Malmö on April 18th, in front of 24,761 visitors. I didn't have money for a ticket but I managed to slip into the game. We won 4–0 and Olle Zetherlund scored a hat trick. It was an almost magical experience, which made a huge impression on me. That seventy-five years later I would also be there when the last match was played at Råsunda feels today like a fairy tale.

It was a really good year. The move to Råsunda, SM gold and then a summer holiday with sun and play awaited. At that time, the football season began in autumn and ended in the spring. I was almost eight years old and for me the sun shone that year, but beyond my horizon the clouds of worry gathered. There was talk of the increasing instability in Europe. In Germany, Adolf Hitler and his National Socialist Party had been in power since 1933 and despite their anti-

Semitic orientation, few could imagine that the world was facing another great war. A war that would cost millions of lives, redraw maps and create scars so deep that they would be passed down for generations to come.

In Åkeshov, I didn't think about Hitler or war. I played football with my friends and fantasised about being Olle Zetherlund, 'Lillis' Persson, 'Tomten' Söderström or any other of the yellow and black heroes who took home the cup. I had no idea of the impending war, nor the fact that the trophy won by my heroes in 1937 would much later be replaced by a trophy named after me. The first trophy was called Von Rosen's trophy after Count Clarence von Rosen. What led to the change was that it emerged that von Rosen had strong ties to the Swedish nationalist movement, which supported the German Nazis, and that he was a personal friend of both Adolf Hitler and Hermann Göring.

2

Hitler and Jesse Owens

The year before AIK's gold and my first match at the Stockholm Stadium, I would be a part of something that I did not realise the historical significance of at the time. In the summer of 1936, I hadn't even had time to turn seven. A school friend called Sven Jonsson, whose mother was German, used to go down every summer to visit relatives in Berlin, which they would also do during the summer of 1936. Sven asked me one day if I wanted to come along. I don't remember exactly what I thought, I guess I was surprised, but I know that at least I said yes at once. What a gigantic adventure, to go abroad! At the same time, I thought that my parents probably wouldn't allow such a thing. That's why I was surprised when they let me go. It was a huge thrill for a six-year-old boy from Åkeshov to take the train from central Stockholm down to Denmark and on to Berlin.

Shortly after we arrived in Berlin, Sven's mother told us that the Olympic Games were being held in the city and wondered if we wanted to go. Both Sven and I were interested in sports, so of course we were overjoyed.

At this time, Hitler was considered to be Germany's saviour, and his energetic speech about order also impressed the Swedes. Especially people employed in the military and the police force fell for Hitler's propaganda, as did my own brother Ernst, who held Hitler as an example. Back then, no one knew what we know now. I remember hearing my brother later say to Dad:

"I was wrong about Hitler, I understand that now."

The Olympic tournament was a great propaganda spectacle for the growing Nazism in Germany. Hitler decided that no Jewish or Roma athletes would be allowed to participate, even if they represented Germany. An exception was made for Helene Mayer who was superior and won gold in fencing. Shortly after the Olympics, when the Nazis began to openly harass and deport Jews, Helene Mayer fled to the United States.

The Olympic Stadium in Berlin was a prestigious building and the games were filmed by Leni Riefenstahl and shown as a documentary entitled *The Great Olympic*. Of course, Hitler gave a grand opening speech, but a Swede also spoke at the opening.

The person who was perhaps the most famous Swede abroad at the time, the explorer Sven Hedin, gave a speech in the arena in Berlin. Through his voyages of discovery in Central Asia, in 1902 he became the last Swede to be ennobled. He was a strong friend of Germany and saw the Soviet Union as the biggest threat in Europe. On several occasions during the war he visited Göring, Hitler and other leading Nazis, but what really tarnished his reputation was the eulogy about Hitler, after his suicide in the bunker, that Sven wrote in *DN* (a Swedish newspaper). He described the dictator as 'one of the greatest men world history has ever seen'. In the final stages of the war, Hedin tried to polish his bad reputation and claimed he used his German contacts to get prisoners out of the concentration camps.

In 1936, no one could predict how the coming Second World War would split Europe and large parts of the rest of the world and that people would later talk about a before and an after.

I sat there in the stands and watched everything wide-eyed. My friend Sven and I watched the historic final in the 100 metres sprint, won by the American Jesse Owens. We didn't think about it at the time - for us it was just an awesome final - but Jesse Owens was African-American and the fact that he won a total of four gold medals in Berlin clearly annoyed Hitler, who wanted to show the superiority of the Aryan race with the Olympics.

When I think back, I can hardly believe what I was involved in. I saw Jesse Owens walking around there, and about a hundred yards away stood Adolf Hitler. The memory is positive, but in retrospect also deeply unpleasant.

Jesse Owens 1936 Olympics Berlin

Hitler at 1936 Olympics

1936 Olympics

3

War and Love

It's hard to remember what I thought about the war when it started: I was so young and much has been coloured by what I later learned about what happened. I have memories of the civil defence exercises on what to do in the event of an attack on Sweden. I remember the intense conversations at home.

Dad was a staunch communist during the war and thought Stalin at least stood for something and got things done. I remember that the press was initially quite Nazi-friendly, which meant that the people could easily be misled. One of the biggest Swedish opponents of the right-wing winds that blew during the war was the theatre director, actor and singer Karl-Gerhard, who among other things wrote 'The Trojan Horse' as a direct resistance song against Hitler and the growing Nazism. As someone interested in music, I also took Karl-Gerhard's and other cultural commentators' criticism to heart.

It was a terrible time in Europe and the world when the war started, on September 1, 1939. I can still see the image of my parents and older siblings sitting and listening intently to crackly radio broadcasts, and the way people on the street were talking. Fragments of anxious conversations and dramatic news broadcasts were like a filter over life, but as a child you didn't understand everything. Would we be drawn into the war? What would happen then? Unclear memories but strong feelings. I remember feelings that life was unfair, and I learned that the horrors of war hit the poor harder than those with money, who can buy an escape route.

The war changed everything. Large parts of Europe lay in ruins, but Sweden, which remained neutral, managed surprisingly better than other countries. Even though we were not directly affected, I had an insight that settled deeply within me: I realised that what you have can be taken away from you. Nothing can be taken for granted.

Sport can give comfort and meaning and for me it had become my greatest passion – and as soon as I could, I went to AIK's matches. On Sundays we often went to church and after that I cycled straight to Råsunda to watch the matches, which in those days started at 1.30pm.

A brutally tangible consequence of the war was that many major footballing nations lost their impact through the death of so many players at the fronts around Europe. England, at this time, was a broken nation, and Sweden offered English teams the chance to come over to Sweden and play matches, helping with training facilities, contacts and equipment. Charlton Athletic, who at this time were considered one of London's great teams, wanted to play a training match against AIK and the date was fixed for 7th June 1946.

As usual, I cycled to Råsunda to see my heroes, where above all Börje Leander was the big star. Before the match, the audience was told that AIK had been loaned Jönköping Södra's top scorer Karl 'Timpa' Simonsson to strengthen the team. In retrospect, it can be concluded that this was a stroke of genius by AIK. The match would later be called the most incredible match of the 20th century by AIK players. But it didn't start well. Charlton literally walked all over AIK and the goals trickled in, one after another.

With less than 30 minutes left in the game, Charlton led by a whopping 7–1 and the crowd began to despair. Then something happened. First, Lennart Pettersson scored a goal, then 'Garvis' Carlsson, and then loaned 'Timpa' went to work and turned the game around with three goals. And then when he also equalised 7–7 in the 89th minute, there was a pure carnival atmosphere in the stands.

We in the audience had to pinch ourselves to understand that it was true. AIK had turned 1–7 into 7–7 and with fourteen goals in one game, no one could complain that they didn't get value for money. I, who had then reached the age of sixteen and had grown into a tall boy, got a memory for life.

"You're not going to go to school for half your life, are you?" Dad said after I finished primary school at Olofslund's Norra Kommunala. But I didn't listen to him and chose to continue with five years of secondary school. The years in real school were fun, but I was not a very good pupil. What I liked the most was playing and joking with my friends. After I took the science exam, my brother Runo, who lived in Gothenburg, got in touch and said he could get me a job down there. Runo himself was a carpenter, but the job he arranged was something completely different.

At the time, sugar and cooking fat were expensive, so an American company had entered the market with a new and cheaper product. The company was called the American Bakery Company and they specialised in sugar and fat substitutes, which were delivered at night to bakeries and restaurants.

I was happy to have a job; the odd working hours were not something I thought about. I hadn't been working there long when rumours began to spread that customers had become ill from eating wheat loaves, cinnamon buns and other things that contained paraffin oil.

The police began to investigate and quickly concluded that it had a connection with the American Bakery Company. When my father Hilmer heard about it, he called Runo and requested that I be sent home to Stockholm immediately.

"We in the Johansson family have never been seen as thieves and it will remain that way," said Father, and I had to head home again.

As it turned out, that was a stroke of luck for me, as otherwise everything might have turned out differently. Besides, it wasn't long until it was time for my military service. Before that, I applied for a job as a warehouse worker at the food company Martin Ohlsson AB at Hötorget.

Chief secretary Anna-Stina Leander was seven years older than me. I immediately noticed that I was attracted to her: when I woke up before work, she was the first one I thought about, and I started planning what I would say to her when we met. She had an open personality that I found very attractive. Later I would find out that she was also the little sister of AIK's big star Börje Leander, and that alone almost felt like an unlikely coincidence, like it was meant to be.

After a company party near Drottningholm, I escorted Anna-Stina all the way to her home in Solna, which must have taken a couple of hours on foot. It was during that long walk that it really clicked between us and we became a couple. It could have been problematic: me, an eighteen-year-old warehouse worker, and she, an executive secretary seven years older, but no one cared. The age difference and our different class backgrounds was no obstacle. Everything felt natural.

During the war, two Olympics had been cancelled, but in 1948 it was time again and not in any city, but in London. The city had been hit hard by the Germans' blitz bombings, which spread death and destruction all around. That the Olympics were to be held again and right there in London was a clear sign of who had won and hope and faith in the future began to spread again.

I had saved up some money that I planned to use to go to London if the Swedish national football team made it to the semi-finals or final. The biggest reason was that three AIK players were superstars in the national team: Sune 'Mona-Lisa' Andersson, who got the nickname because he smiled so sneakily, Henry 'Garvis' Karlsson, left winger and Råsunda's top scorer, and my new brother-in-law, the elegant right-back Börje Leander, who came to spend a full fifteen seasons in the AIK shirt and who would mean an enormous amount to my career in sports. A career that I could not even have imagined in my wildest dreams at the time.

There were many nations that cancelled because of the war, but Sweden's effort must still be counted as a feat. I eagerly followed the start of the tournament on the radio and through the newspapers. After Sweden's big win with 12-0 against South Korea, I bought a train ticket and planned the trip by train and boat, which would take just over three days. Tickets for the Olympic football could be bought in some tobacconists. I took a chance and bought a ticket for the final as well. Our neighbour Denmark awaited us in the semi-finals. With Sweden leading 3–1, Gunnar Nordahl ran with such speed that he didn't stop until he was in the net, and then AIK's Henry 'Garvis' Karlsson took the opportunity to score the decisive fourth goal. The match ended 4–2.

I arrived in London on the same day that it was clear that Sweden would face Yugoslavia in the final. A Yugoslavia that was then considered one of Europe's best national teams. I hurried to the arena and as I walked around looking for my seat the Swedish national anthem was heard from the loudspeakers. There was a magical atmosphere at Wembley, an Olympic final in a London that had just begun to rise after a harsh war. I never thought that Sweden would win. But they did. Yugoslavia played at the top of their ability, but Sweden managed, with solid teamwork, to beat back the Yugoslavs, and via goals from two of Sweden's best players of all time, Gunnar Gren and Gunnar Nordahl, the final score was 3–1 to Sweden.

There I stood among 60,000 people in the stands and tried to take in what I understood to be an historic moment. Maybe that's when a seed was planted in me. In the murmur, the jubilation and the tributes, maybe it was there that I unconsciously decided that this atmosphere, this environment, this arena, would be my place in life.

Yugoslavia and Sweden football final at 1948 Olympics

The year after the Olympics, specifically in June 1949, it was time to put on the Crown's green clothes and do military service. With the war so close behind us, it felt natural to do the military year that is expected of all male Swedes. Many Stockholmers were placed in Kiruna or Boden, but I ended up at Svea lifeguard in Stockholm, which I was very happy with because I was then close to Anna-Stina's home, whom I met as soon as I got my first leave. After almost half a year in the army, I turned twenty and got leave of absence, and then I proposed to Anna-Stina who, to my great joy, accepted.

I enjoyed military life and the camaraderie, and I began to notice that I too could be a leader – not that I sought it, but it often came naturally. I was promoted to staff furrier with responsibility for post number one at the Royal Palace, which meant guarding the outer court and the colonnade.

Military life also meant a lot of sports and outdoor activities, and I shared a hatch with several future Allsvenskan players. I decided to play football myself and I was okay, but I knew that I didn't have what it took to reach the top.

I felt grown up now. I was in command of the post and engaged to the love of my life.

Out in society, hope for the future slowly began to grow.

4

AIK Relegated; But Happiness in my Private Life

My parents were both completely uninterested in sports and you probably couldn't say that I was encouraged to get as involved as I did. Now, in retrospect, I sometimes think that there was a desire for revenge in me that was spurred on by their lack of encouragement: I wanted to show them what I could do.

AIK was, in the late 1940s, an established top team in the top Swedish league, the Allsvenskan. My brother-in-law Börje Leander, Sune 'Mona-Lisa' Andersson and Gösta 'Pröjsarn' Nilsson were the leading players. One of the most legendary transitions in Swedish football history took place in the autumn of 1949 when Hammarby's gold nugget, the later legendary Lennart 'Nacka' Skoglund, transferred to the Rats. AIK had had eyes on him for a long time, even though he played in division two. He signed the contract for a thousand Swedish kronor, an overcoat and a rag rug to put on the kitchen floor at his parents' home on Katarina Bangata in Södermalm.

Nacka was not ready to play until after the World Cup break in 1950, a World Cup in which Sweden took bronze.

In the 1949/50 season, AIK had the best attendance figures in the club's history, with an average attendance of 21,768 – the record was not broken until 2018, when the average attendance was 23,664. A friendly match against the big Italian club Milan was seen by around 40,000 people and AIK won by 3 –1.

However, things did not go as well during an England tour when there were three straight losses against Chelsea,

Liverpool and a total of 0-8 against Arsenal. With the new acquisition Nacka in the team, it started well with gold in the Swedish Cup. Then no one saw the clouds on the horizon. AIK had since the start been a founder member of the Allsvenskan, and the only team allowed to play at the national arena, and the risk that they would leave was considered very small. Perhaps they should have waited to sell Nacka, who had already signed a contract with Italian Inter after five games. Many of AIK's leading players were on the brink of being too old, and panic had began to creep into the team. Falling down the league table happened quickly.

Theodor 'Thodde' Malm, once one of AIK's most important players, became seriously ill during the year and on his sickbed said the ominous words: "AIK can handle this, we have never gone out of the league table, we are too good for that." An hour later he died, only sixty years old.

After a miserable end to the season, it was clear that we were being relegated, for the first time ever. For me, it was the first time that I had had to endure the bitter feelings of being the loser. I could be extremely disappointed when things went badly for AIK.

On a personal level, something more positive would happen that would have a big impact on my life. Once again it was fate and coincidence that played a role.

One of my friends had a pregnant girlfriend and when it was time for her to give birth, I was the one who had to borrow one of the company's jeeps to drive the nervous expectant father to the hospital.

It would turn out to be a false alarm, but since the birth was still expected to take place in the next few days, I had to stay a few days in Stockholm, waiting to be able to drive my friend back to our military accommodation afterwards. Of course, I took the opportunity to visit my family in Åkeshov and it was when I was flipping through the newspaper that I saw an advertisement with the headline 'Linoleum AB Forshaga seeks junior salesman'. The ad caught my eye and I thought it sounded like it could be something for me, so I called, and was offered an interview right away.

The company was based in Gothenburg but also had an office in Stockholm, and that was where the job interviews were held.

Without a second thought that I should perhaps change my clothes, I went there in the military's green uniform, something that did not go unnoticed.

"Why are you wearing military clothes?" said the man who was to conduct the interview in surprise. I freaked out at first because I hadn't even thought about it, but then I told the story of my friend with his pregnant fiancée. Perhaps that was what decided it all. I noticed that the man's eyes smiled and his face opened up as I told him.

A few days later the phone rang and I was told that I had got the job. I would start immediately after I was finished in the army.

That job would be decisive for me, and when much later I was the CEO and went through old employment interviews, I found my own and saw the note: 'Definitely the best guy.' With a smile I thought back to that time.

AIK was thus relegated and would play in division two north-east. Their coach was the Englishman George Raynor, who had enjoyed great success with the Swedish national team: Olympic gold in 1948 and World Cup bronze in 1950. He was now joined by Per 'Pära' Kaufeldt, who during his time as a player was called 'Football's Napoleon' for his unique ability to be extremely dangerous at the same time as being the team's great playmaker. He is still AIK's top scorer of all time with his 122 goals in 170 games. This was what AIK needed. Their season became impressive when they secured victory already at the beginning of October. The Rats were back!

The work as a junior salesperson at AB Forshaga Linoleum suited me well. I put my social skills to good use – I've always found it easy to talk to people. I also got on well with my co-workers. It wasn't just in my life that everything was better - what had begun stealthily after the war, had by the beginning of the 50s blossomed into full bloom: an unheard-of faith in the future. I can't remember any other time that was as positive as Sweden in the 1950s. People were more open and happier than they'd been in a long time. I became good friends with Anna-Stina's brother and we had a lot of fun together and hung out often, sometimes with Garvis, another great player. AIK were back where they belonged: in the Allsvenskan. Life felt very good. I alternated work and family with matches at Råsunda. Anna-Stina and I were engaged and were soon to be married.

5

Family, Advancement and a New Friendship

I almost knew the lyrics by heart after all the times I'd heard it played on the radio:

> ... He flew, he flew, until the twilight of the evening came,
> he turned repentantly to the rose.
> He wanted to beg, what he just missed,
> a bed of purple and a queen's kiss...

The song was called 'Rosen och fjärilen' – 'The Rose and the Butterfly' - and was played all the time in 1954; it was a bit of a national scourge. The singer was none other than AIK's goal-dangerous forward Ingvar 'Tjotta' Olsson. The single would sell a whopping 90,000 copies and Tjotta alternated matches in the Allsvenskan with performances in public parks. It was said that Tjotta used to tune in to sing almost any time, whether it was in the dressing room or at a party. He was not a one-hit-wonder but later achieved great success as an artist.

As often as the job allowed, I followed Tjotta's and AIK's progress, and the job as a salesperson at Forshaga also meant many trips around Sweden.

When we got married, Anna-Stina and I moved to an apartment in Hässelby, not far from my childhood home. The age difference and our different class backgrounds were not noticed when our families celebrated our wedding. It was a very nice moment, and when I looked at her I saw my future.

I was content with my life. At work I was appreciated and quite quickly I was promoted to senior salesman, which meant better pay but also meant more travelling. But the biggest thing of all was that Anna-Stina became pregnant. I'll never forget when I found out; I felt warm all over. I was going to be a father, I could hardly believe it was true, one of the greatest things you can be a part of. The child was due in the spring of 1955 and an eager wait began. Anna-Stina's stomach grew so fast that you could almost see it expanding. Time passed quickly but slowly at the same time and was filled for me with work and football, football, football.

Kurre Hamrin 1958

During these years, it was above all two young guys who distinguished themselves in AIK and both of them had with the nickname 'Kurre'. Kurre Liander was brilliant and with his technical and forward play he opened up spaces for the always dangerous Kurre Hamrin, who became a real legend.

Hamrin's ability to score goals quickly made foreign clubs aware of him. Italian giants Juventus got in touch and were clearly interested in bringing Kurre to Turin. In the end, the clubs came to an agreement: Kurre would be allowed to play in AIK for half the season before he moved to Italy, and you really can't complain about his farewell performances. In the twelve games that Kurre managed during the season, he netted a total of thirteen times. When he said goodbye to his beloved AIK, he had delivered a whopping 53 goals in 62 games in the yellow and black shirt.

I followed Kurre Hamrin's breakthrough with great interest and still believe today that he is one of the best footballers who ever played for AIK.

Then the time finally came. On April 12, 1955, Anna-Stina gave birth to our first child. It was a daughter whom we named Eva Maria. All the women in my family had Maria as their middle name. Life changed, especially for Anna-Stina, who had the most responsibility; it was just the way things were at that time, it wasn't something you even thought about. It got crowded in the apartment in Hässelby and we started looking around for something else. We both thought that Solna was a good alternative and besides, it was close to Råsunda, which within a few years would prove to be a good choice.

The job at Forshaga took up a lot of my time and I gained more and more trust from the managers. As often happens, the man takes on more work and the woman takes care of the children and the home, and thus the world they previously shared slowly begins to drift apart and become two different ones. It wasn't something I thought about at the time, but that's just the way things were back then.

In order to continue to advance in the company, I realised that I needed to improve my language skills and therefore started taking evening courses in English and German: one more thing that would prove to be very important in the future. Sometimes it worried me that there wasn't enough time. It was not easy being a travelling salesman and at the same time being a present father. Those years were very busy, and I wonder how I managed everything. A lot of work, a lot of travelling, the evening studies and many dinners with clients.

Anna-Stina's brother Börje Leander visited often and he told us a lot of funny things about football. He told me during a dinner that the apparently dangerous back passes he sometimes used to do were rehearsed, as a trick to entertain the crowd.

There used to be a buzz through the audience when Börje, with his back to his own goal, hit a hard back pass that forced the keeper Gurra Sjöberg to throw himself at the ball to avoid an own goal. I thought things like that were extremely funny.

It was an intense period in my life and in addition our family was to be expanded with our second daughter Lena, who was born on 11 April 1957.

Major changes awaited in the Allsvenskan. The season, which was played autumn–spring, was changed in 1957/58 to spring–autumn. The reason was above all due to the weather. It was felt that both spectators and players would find better conditions to both play and watch football during the warmer months of the year. Another thing that influenced the decision was that the European Cup had recently started, which opened new doors for Swedish teams to measure their strength against major European teams.

Behind the first European Cup was the French sports newspaper *L'Équipe*, which made UEFA a proposal on how such a cup should be played. For that reason, the first European Cup final was played in Paris on June 13, 1956. Real Madrid, with the notorious goal scorer Di Stéfano on top form, lifted the first European Cup trophy after the final victory against the French Stade de Reims. Djurgården represented Sweden in the first edition of the European Cup and made it to the quarter-finals.

Something very big in terms of Swedish sport was that Sweden was to host the 1958 football World Cup. Sweden was also considered to have a good chance of performing well, not only because they played well at home but also because Sweden had a generation of players who had all made themselves known in Europe: Lennart 'Nacka' Skoglund, Gunnar Gren, Nils Liedholm, Kurre Hamrin and Bror Mellberg, who returned to AIK.

Swedish Squad 1958 FIFA World Cup
From left: Kurt Hamrin, Reino Börjesson, Orvar Bergmark, Kalle Svensson, Sven Axbom and Sigge Parling. Standing from left: Lennart "Nacka" Skoglund, Gunnar Gren, Agne Simonsson, Bengt "Julle" Gustavsson and Nils "Il Barone" Liedholm.

Before the World Cup, I worked for a few weeks down at the head office in Gothenburg and I heard that Brazil was training on the football pitches at Hindås, just outside Gothenburg. I had heard a lot about Brazil's way of playing football, about the technique and the artistry, so I went there to catch a glimpse of the stars. Brazil were tipped to win the entire championship, and there were many famous players in the team that came to Sweden in the summer of 1958. Names like

Nílton Santos, Didi, Gilmar, Vavá and Garrincha had created something that in their home country was called samba football.

The year 1958 was a completely different time to now. Back then, there were no security guards or police to keep the crowd away from practices, so I could get right up to the fence next to the field where they were training. I had heard about, above all, one young guy who would be something special. He was predicted to be the world's best player and of course I wanted to see that. I stood there looking through the loops of the fence and saw a young guy juggling the ball with incredible technique, putting it on his neck before letting it drop and then passing it to another player. Wow, I thought as I stood there gaping, this guy is really good.

There weren't that many of us standing there watching and he must have noticed how I was looking at him because after a while the lanky boy came up to me and said hello. I can't remember what we said to each other, but I do remember that we somehow managed to hold a conversation, him in Portuguese and me in half-broken English.

We introduced ourselves to each other and I told him that my name was Lennart Johansson and I remember that I thought his name sounded long and complicated. He was seventeen years old and his name was Edson Arantes do Nascimento, but he is much better known as Pelé.

Never in my wildest imagination could I have known that the meeting at Hindås sports ground was the beginning of a lifelong friendship.

6

Unforgettable Goals and Political Quarrels

The World Cup in Sweden in 1958 was not only big for football, but also for television. They went hand in hand. The World Cup was the big event that caused television to break through throughout the country. The Swedish national team's great success in the competition obviously contributed to the television hysteria in Sweden. No one expected that Sweden would make it all the way to the World Cup final.

With the television broadcasts, we received classic images that have become etched in our minds. Perhaps the most spectacular was Kurre Hamrin's 'go-goal' where he seemingly easily walked with the ball from the corner and with a few small jerks got past all the West Germans before scoring from a tight angle to make it 3-1 to Sweden. The goal also meant advancement to the World Cup final.

Although the 1958 World Cup is mostly remembered as a big football party where Sweden and Brazil were carried forward by an enthusiastic audience, there was also a fight in the background that went all the way up to a high political level. It was about something as trivial as Sweden's cheerleaders, i.e. the people who had the task of warming up the audience to get a good atmosphere in the arena. Sweden's cheerleaders were named Lennart Nilsson and Håkan Westergren and both were praised for their work at the start of the tournament, but everything changed during the semi-final against West Germany.

It was a good draw for the crowd during the match at Nya Ullevi, thanks in large part to Lennart and Håkan, who whipped up the atmosphere in the stands. The Swedish team enjoyed the support and they dominated the first part of the match despite the Germans taking the lead. Before the end of the half, however, Nacka Skoglund had managed to equalise, and it was when the German defender Erich Juskowiak was sent off that the problems for the Germans began. The Swedish crowd breathed morning air - as we say in Sweden when things are looking up - and began to get their hopes up that we could beat the Germans. For the Germans, it only got worse when their captain Fritz Walter was injured and had to be carried off the field. With only nine men against Sweden's eleven, the Germans were easy prey and after Gunnar Gren's shot on the crossbar from twenty-five metres and Kurre Hamrin's goal, Sweden won the match comfortably.

The Germans' disappointment after the match was not directed at their own performance but at the Swedish cheerleaders. German newspapers wrote about a Swedish conspiracy against the reigning world champions, West Germany. Lennart and Håkan were singled out as instigators and everything escalated in a smear campaign that led to bizarre events. There were rumours that Swedish tourists in Munich were insulted by the local population, that a Swedish flag was torn down at an equestrian competition in Aachen, and that petrol stations in Kiel were asked not to sell petrol to Swedes. Although the German embassy in Stockholm tried to quell the increasingly disproportionate anger, the Germans continued to show their displeasure in their homeland. It escalated so far that the chairman of the German Football Association, Peco Bauwens, announced that West Germany would never play a match against Sweden again. It was a promise he kept during his time as chairman of the Association.

A few years after the World Cup, when emotions had subsided and most had forgotten the dispute, or realised that it was due to pure disappointment, a symbolic friendly match against Sweden was organised in November 1963, which marked the end of the improbable conflict. It was an example of the enormous emotions that football stirs up and of how sport sometimes becomes politics, something that I myself would become aware of later.

The World Cup tournament created new heroes, who gave football a completely different status than it had before. If anyone thought it was excessive then, of course it can't even be compared to today's multi-billion dollar industry.

I was a married father of two and had been promoted to sales manager, which meant that instead of travelling around myself, I had been given responsibility for a group of salespeople. In my free time I hung out with my brother-in-law Börje Leander and also with Garvis, who was employed at Rydholm's menswear shop. There is a very special story about Rydholm's menswear shop. Rydholm's is the reason why AIK and the London club Arsenal have become what they call friendly clubs. Shortly after the Second World War, Arsenal came to visit to play a friendly match against AIK.

England, badly damaged in the war, had just tried to restart the league, but resources were scarce. Arsenal wanted to play practice games and made it clear that they did not need to be paid. However, Putte Kock, who was AIK's then chairman of both the main board and the football board, thought that the English players looked very worn out, as did their clothes. Also, Putte felt it was only right that the English should get something for the game as they were the big reason why so many people came. Therefore, he offered all the players, plus coaches and others in Arsenal's staff, to go down to Rydholm's menswear shop on Kungsholmen and get shoes, shirts, suits and ties. What a sight it must have been, a whole horde of bedraggled Englishmen shopping at the fine store.

Putte Kock is a true legend. His real name was Jonas Rudolf E:son Kock and at first he was called 'Rulle', but when he debuted as the second youngest ever in the Swedish national team, his teammates renamed him 'Putte'. But it wasn't just as a player that Putte made a name for himself. As captain of the national team, he helped win gold in the 1948

Olympics, bronze in the 1950 World Cup and bronze in the 1952 Olympics.

That someone would become more associated with AIK in the future was considered unlikely. Putte sat for thirteen years as chairman of AIK's main board. No one, least of all myself, could believe that I would later be sitting there a year longer than him.

7

Stepping Up

As a youngster, I enjoyed playing both bandy (a popular sport in Sweden, similar to ice hockey) and football, but it wasn't as a player that I wanted to make my mark. Despite my modest active career, I played in several interesting games. Among other things, I remember a raven (the Swedish name for non-league or Sunday league) football match. Before the match, I spoke to another guy whose name was also Lennart but who was called 'Nacka'. We had met before so we were somewhat familiar. The match was between a team of employees at Forshaga and a neighbourhood gang from Södermalm, which for the day was reinforced with Nacka Skoglund. It was on a gravel field below Långholmen prison, I remember. I think Nacka liked me, because before the match he came up and asked what position I would play in.

"I'm often placed as a right-back," I answered.

"I also play on the right side," he replied.

So, he wouldn't be on my side. It was probably because he didn't want to embarrass me and make me look bad in front of my co-workers.

When I stopped playing myself, it did not mean that I lost interest in the sport; it was still my greatest passion. It was through sports that I came to appreciate associational life and how it led to meetings between people from different backgrounds. That people got involved in associations was in many ways a basis for democracy and participation in society. It was something I carried with me throughout my career.

During the late 50s I was not formally active at AIK, but through my circle of friends I was very familiar with how the association worked and what was happening. At the beginning of the 60s, however, something happened that would mean major changes.

It was in bandy that everything began in earnest. My brother-in-law Börje Leander, like many other players at the time, had been active in football, bandy and hockey before he became a star in football. But after an active football career, he became increasingly involved in AIK's bandy section. We hung out and he was very much aware of my interest and commitment to AIK and that I had leadership experience at Forshaga. One day he asked me if I would consider sitting on the board of the bandy section. It was a great honour.

Actually, I was busy, to say the least, with work at Forshaga and with my family. I weighed it back and forth but pretty quickly landed on it being such an honour that I had to accept.

Previously, bandy had been prioritised over hockey. But when television caught on, hockey became more interesting and gained a higher status than bandy, which did not work as well on television. It meant that some of our best bandy players were lured over to hockey and it caused AIK to lose its place in the top league. At that time there were no real contracts and some players devoted themselves to football, bandy and hockey. When I joined the board, AIK bandy was in a difficult situation.

AIK football also had problems in the early 60s and was close to the unpleasant relegation zone already in the 1960 season, but managed to finish in sixth place after an impressive sprint. The following year it got worse. The twenty-two-year-old talent Kurt Andersson was AIK's main attack weapon, together with Lennart Backman, but Italian clubs saw this and it didn't take long before Udinese came up with an offer that was surprising at the time. A whopping SEK 180,000 was offered, and that meant Kurt Andersson was lost to Italy. The season ended with the team leaving the Allsvenskan in 1961 for the second time in its history. I had by then gone from being a member to becoming chairman of the bandy section.

When the football team managed to get up to the highest league again, help came from bandy. The rescue came when bandy section member and bandy player Sören Häggström scored the decisive goal against IS Halmia, which meant that AIK were ready for promotion, but with only a one-goal margin. It was fun and I enjoyed myself, and it also seemed that I was liked by the players and managers at the club. Bruno Nyberg and Lennart Hemming in AIK football got in touch and wanted a meeting.

Nyberg was known to be a very determined and harsh man, I remember. He was not easy to get along with and sometimes his stubbornness and grumpiness went into overdrive. But I learned over time to respond to his whims in such a way that he thought he was in charge, while we were doing the opposite of what he wanted. The meeting was very short. They told me they wanted me over at AIK football and I said yes without hesitation.

Everything went so fast during this time. One thing led to another. I remember being overjoyed to be asked. That I, Lennart Johansson from Åkeshov and an AIK member since I was a little boy watching Gurra Sjöberg excel in the goal, would get a seat on the AIK football board was a big deal. Almost unimaginable. I kept a serious straight face in the meeting, but as soon as I got out into the street, I felt my face break into a big smile and I wanted to shout out my joy. At the next board meeting I was elected as a member of AIK football's board, and this was the start of a long journey for me in the world of football.

Beneath all the joy there was also something else. At first it was just a faint, almost imperceptible feeling. Over time it grew stronger. I had a family and two small children at home. How would I be enough? I really didn't want to be an absentee father, but no matter what I did, there was never enough time.

8

Knocked Out by Ingo and a Dear Reunion

We sat among the allotments at Brommaplan in western Stockholm to have dinner outside. It was a fine summer day in 1963. The man sitting next to me is considered one of Sweden's greatest boxing athletes ever. In 1959 at the Yankee Stadium in New York, Ingemar 'Ingo' Johansson knocked out American Floyd Patterson seven times in the third round. Ingo then became heavyweight world champion. The atmosphere was cheerful and we'd drunk a couple of schnapps shots. We'd met for the first time in Gothenburg a few years earlier during a football match; Ingo was a blue and white IFK Gothenburg supporter.

As he was now visiting Stockholm, we had decided to meet and have dinner together with our wives. I don't remember whose idea it was, after a few beers and a number of shots, to rope up a makeshift boxing ring. Ingo, who was at the end of his career, had been given a few weeks off from training and agreed to show me some of the swings and hooks that had won him the championship. I don't know how I dared, but I said yes when Ingo asked if I wanted to spar. Ingo had a feared right hand which journalists called Thor's hammer.

Ingemar Johansson 1960

At first I thought it went really well and we tripped around each other in the ring while mostly marking jabs. Then I just remember that Ingo said,

"Now you, Lennart."

Then it went black.

When I opened my eyes again I saw the clouds above me, and then Ingo, with a smile, asked if I wanted help getting up. I felt my body shake as he held out his hand and pulled me back to my feet. Just then I wondered what the hell I was doing; but now I think, well, not everyone has been knocked out by Ingo.

I became increasingly involved in AIK football's board in the role of chairman. After a few difficult years, the club had begun to climb up the table, both sportingly and in terms of audience, as the audience also found its way back to Råsunda. Through my work at Forshaga, I had built up a good network of contacts with widely different people, and that would be very significant. It was an exciting AIK that was tipped to finish high in the table ahead of the 1964 season. In addition to 'Liston' Söderberg, who was known for his explosive temper, they had strengthened the squad with IS Halmia's striker Lars Sjöström. It was also time for a player who would become one of AIK's most faithful of all time to make an entrance: Jim Nildén. Despite looking so promising, the team only achieved seventh place that season, which was disappointing. The performances were too uneven and we agreed that reinforcement was needed - this was when my network of contacts came in handy. Through my friend the sports journalist Bobby Byström at *Dagens Nyheter* newspaper, I had received a tip about a player who was interested in a change of environment, and it wasn't just any player. Actually, it was Fiskar-Owe's wife who wanted a change of environment, while he himself was quite satisfied with his existence as top scorer at IFK Gothenburg. The nickname Fiskar (Fisherman) came from the fact that he was born on the coast outside Gothenburg, where the fishing industry was the main occupation.

Owe had spent nine years at IFK Gothenburg, 165 games and 101 goals in the Allsvenskan, which places him in fifth place among IFK's best scorers of all time. And he probably would have continued if his wife hadn't wanted to move to Stockholm. My friend Bobby Byström had found out about this, and I realised that it meant an opportunity to tie a really big player to the club. It wasn't entirely uncontroversial, but I thought it was worth a shot. I contacted an engineering agency that was a customer I had met through Forshaga and they agreed to give him a job. After that I started trying to persuade Owe. It wasn't easy, but I didn't give up. Owe was probably quite flattered that AIK did so much to get him to the club, and in the end he agreed.

Owe Ohlsson paid dividends immediately. With twelve goals and an impressive game, Owe took The Rats to the top position. The 1965 season featured many memorable games, but the one that will forever live on is the battering of Hammarby away from home. When the referee blew the whistle, it was 1-8 on the scoreboard. Owe had scored four of the goals. Fiskar-Owe is perhaps my best signing ever, I think now. He was good both on and off the pitch.

I don't know if it was due to my initiative with the signing, but it became clear that I was being given an increasingly important role in the club during 1966. More players came to the club that year, including the later famous coach Tord Grip from Degerfors.

Another big profile player was Roland Lundblad, who was called 'Rimbo'. He took the Swedish league by storm: some journalists called him a prankster, while others said he was uncorrupted, cheerful and optimistic.

Pele 1960 Malmö Stadium

What made 1966 an extra important year for me was that I got to meet my Brazilian friend Pelé again. The World Cup finals in England awaited and through some contacts it was decided that AIK would be allowed to face Brazil's World Cup team in a training match. We borrowed foreign professional Kurre Hamrin to be able to match Brazil's star-studded national team. Right from the start, it felt like a match out of the ordinary, when Pelé almost immediately after kick-off lobbed the ball over AIK's goalkeeper Gunnar Lund, who was too far out to be able to reach it. A whoosh went through the crowd as the ball hit the crossbar. The Brazilians eventually won 4–2. Pelé recognised me when I went to their training facility and we started talking about everything. He and I clicked.

New tasks also awaited me when I was elected as the new chairman of AIK's main board. In my world I had now reached as high as it was possible to get. To be the highest representative of AIK was the biggest thing I could ever dream of.

Now Dad would be proud, I said quietly to myself.

9

The Start of My Career in the Top Job at AIK

My father Hilmer and mother Maria were largely uninterested in football, and as I climbed the hierarchy they followed me with a certain scepticism. They obviously thought that the work at Forshaga was much more important than the jobs in football. Maybe that's why I chose to stay with the company for so long, even though football was taking up more and more of my time.

I don't remember them ever expressing admiration for what I did in football; they never talked about it. But I lived with the notion that they would be proud, if only they understood how important sport could be and how far it can take you. For me, their lack of interest has been a driving force, I understand now, although I hardly felt it at the time.

That's the way it is, you always seek confirmation from your parents no matter how successful you are. They were from another time. I was sloppy and they were probably worried how it would go for "the little boy".

Sometimes when I've met famous people I've found myself thinking about my parents. One such occasion was when I met Prime Minister Olof Palme. He came up to me after an AIK match at Råsunda and asked what I thought of Jimpa Nildén. I admired Olof Palme and his leadership and used to say that he had only one fault: he was a Djurgården football team supporter. Olof Palme said that he had studied Jim Nildén's way of holding and protecting the ball and concluded that he destroyed the rhythm of the game. I nodded in response.

On one hand, I thought: how much of an a Djurgården supporter are you really when you spend so much time and effort studying an AIK player? On the other hand, I understood that Prime Minister Palme knew more about football than I thought.

There was a love-hate relationship between the Stockholm clubs. Something we worked with was the Stockholm Alliance, an association that was formed as early as 1948 and consisted of the capital's three big clubs: AIK, Djurgården and Hammarby. As a member of AIK's football board, I was already invited to represent the club in the Alliance, which apart from me consisted of Lennart Nyman for Hammarby and Gunnar Lundkvist for Djurgården.

The idea behind the Alliance was that the clubs' representatives could meet and discuss joint events, players or whatever came up. We held pleasant meetings and dinners, but in the back of our minds we all knew that we would try to deceive each other in order to give our own club advantages. Nyman was the most cunning of us. One event would almost mean the dissolution of the Alliance.

It was an unwritten but clear rule not to bid for or try to sign a player with whom one of the other Alliance clubs had already begun negotiations. Back then, in the mid-60s, the players did not have salaries or benefits comparable to today's contracts. Instead, it was usually about which job or home a club could attract.

Djurgården, with Gunnar Lundkvist at the helm, had for some time shown interest in Landskrona BoIS' Dan Brzokoupil, and after much back and forth it seemed as if Dan was ready to move from Skåne to Stockholm to play for the blue stripes. Djurgården had arranged work and housing and also an unknown transitional sum, which for that time was very high. You could say that the only thing missing was Dan's name on the contract so that everything would be completely clear and he would formally belong to Djurgården. Only days before everything was to be locked down, he was instead contacted by Hammarby's Lennart Nyman, who had somehow managed to scrape together money that trumped Djurgården's sum. Obviously, the shit hit the fan when it came out how things had gone down. Dan Brzokoupil became Södermalm's favourite and was forever hated by the Djurgården supporters.

My first two years as chairman of AIK football involved many crisis meetings, as the sporting part had clear shortcomings. After starting the 1967 season with several victories, the end of the season was just the opposite. It was clear that we needed to strengthen the places in the team where the deficiencies were most evident. Already during the season, two new acquisitions had arrived that would be important to the club. Curt Edenvik came from Degerfors and would be the last in history to represent the club in the Swedish national league in both football and hockey at the same time. It was a balancing act that become increasingly difficult the more football developed. A very clear example was when Curt first played in the Allsvenskan last round of the season against Malmö and then had one hour and forty-five minutes to get ready for the hockey match against Tegs SK at Hovet.

Olavus Olsson was recruited from Högalid and had the nickname 'Olka'. Before the 1968 season, Olka heard that several others in the team had signed some kind of contract and he wanted to meet someone from the board to discuss whether he was also eligible for one.

At this time all contracts were signed with the main board. Olka was a little unlucky because he had to meet the notoriously grumpy and sometimes mean Bruno Nyberg to present his case. Bruno had some days when he was impossible to talk to. To Olka's question about contracts, the answer was a resounding no.

"Why not?" wondered Olka.

"Because I say so," said Bruno, even more sourly, if that was at all possible.

So Olka had to leave without a contract or pre-clearance. I later made sure that Olka also got his contract. I don't know if Bruno ever found out.

10

The Greatest Football Player Retires

Time went by at breakneck speed, and the 60s turned into the 70s. For me, the early 70s were a fun time when the board and players hung out and it felt like everyone was pulling in the same direction.

Football underwent a slow transformation. Two trends could be discerned: on the one hand money began to gain more and more importance in the sport, and on the other hand supporters in certain areas became increasingly aggressive. It was on a small scale and you could never imagine what it would be like a couple of decades later. Liverpool's legendary coach Bill Shankly once said: "Some people say that football is about life and death. I don't like that attitude, I can assure you that it's much more important than that." In any case, it was during these years that the hooligan culture slowly began to emerge.

1970 was a World Cup year and this time it was Mexico who hosted the competition. Sweden, after missing two World Cup finals in a row, had managed to qualify, and ended up in the same group as Italy, Israel and Uruguay. After losing 1–0 to Italy in the opener on 3rd June, Sweden played four days later against Israel in a match that ended 1–1.

Despite a 1–0 win against Uruguay on June 11th, it was not enough for further advancement for Sweden. With only two goals scored and as many conceded, Uruguay took second place in the group behind Italy, by a goal margin.

But the World Cup in Mexico in 1970 was still something very special for me because it was the last big performance for one of my close friends and role models in the world of football.

Pelé, who took both Sweden and the rest of the world by storm in the 1958 World Cup, was playing his last tournament. After the big fiasco in 1966, when Brazil didn't even advance from the group, they wanted revenge. The final was a showdown between two of the greatest nations in football history: Brazil and Italy. A total of 107,412 people were in attendance at the Azteca Stadium in Mexico City, and eighteen minutes into the first half the entire stadium exploded as Pelé gave Brazil a 1-0 lead.

Brazil national team 1970
Front row left to right: Jairzinho, Rivelino, Tostao, Pelé, Paulo Cézar Caju.
Back row left to right: Carlos Alberto, Brito, Piazza, Felix, Clodoaldo, Everaldo.

Led by Pelé, they scored three more goals and the final ended 4–1. Brazil's third World Cup was salvaged. Personally, I was especially happy that Pelé got such a nice and dignified end to his legendary career at the very highest level. To this day, he is the only player with three World Cup gold medals. He played his last international match the following year at the

Maracanã Stadium in Rio de Janeiro, Brazil. In my eyes, he is the greatest soccer player of all time.

But even though Pelé's national team career was over, that didn't mean we wouldn't see each other again. Twenty-five years later, when I faced my toughest battle in international football, Pelé was one of my main pillars of support.

11

Total Football and an Approaching Disaster

There was optimism in the air. The 1970s began with a policy of détente between the USA and the Soviet Union. 1972 saw the tenth manned space flight and the fifth landing on the moon. The same year would be one of AIK's best years for a long time, thanks in large part to the new acquisitions the club made.

The twins Yngve and Börje Leback from Älvsjö and Dag Szepanski from Malmö were now also joined by a tough, energetic and hard-working midfielder from Ludvika named Rolf Zetterlund. But one of the most important players in the successful year of 1972 came from their own ranks. Gerry Rehn is one of the few players in the club's history who has represented AIK in all teams, from the youngest boys' team up to senior level. The team did well and almost made it all the way. The only loss of the season was against Öster and that was enough for Åtvidaberg to clinch the gold by a margin of one point.

As I was now also CEO at Forshaga, I had created a large network of contacts all over Sweden which also came in handy when it came to my assignments in the sports world. That way I could justify to myself keeping all the assignments at the same time. It was good. But somewhere under there were my parents' urging voices about having a 'real job'.

At AIK I felt valued. Many AIK players called me 'Johan'; I don't remember exactly why, but I think it was because the name Johansson was so common. In addition to the job at Forshaga, I had several different roles within AIK. I remained on the bandy's board a few years after being recruited to the football board, then I became chairman of the football section and then it wasn't long before I was elected chairman of AIK's main board. Everything was like in a dream, it just happened in one go. When I became chairman of the main board, I had to pinch myself to understand that it was true. We had great fun at work. There was also very good cohesion between managers and players at that time, and we often hung out in our spare time, and went on trips together, which created a family atmosphere. The main board had a completely different function in the 70s than it does now. Every signing of players in those days had to be approved by the main board and we had a closer cooperation with the various sections.

Another board member was the old goalkeeper hero Börje Fridlund, who was a dentist by profession. That could be good to have within the club as it wasn't uncommon for teeth to come loose when players nodded together. Also on the board, he had the title "treasurer", which actually meant that he was bursar. The person who acted as an agent on behalf of the board and looked for new talent was Ingemar Ingevik, who was originally a trained physical education teacher. We used to go with the team on training camps and match tours and I think the cohesion was also the great strength of the club. It felt like everyone was involved and contributed and felt the value in what they were doing.

We are Swedish football boys
We know that the road to the World Cup is difficult...

So began the song that made it all the way to the top in Sweden before the World Cup in 1974. It was written by George 'Åby' Ericson who was also the national team coach and who before the World Cup combined his two interests: football and music. Since 1970, Åby had been the first full-time national team manger. The World Cup in West Germany in 1974 was part of Sweden's return to football's elite. We managed to progress from the group stage but went out after a classic match against West Germany which we lost 4–2, but where the image of Ralf

Edström's outstretched arm after a magnificent volley into the roof of the net would live on forever.

The fact that Ralf coolly stretched a hand in the air, despite the beautiful goal, was due, according to his own statement, to the fact that he had an upset stomach the day before and would have risked pooping his pants if he ran around and celebrated - true or not, a good story should never be questioned and it looked cheeky.

In addition to Sweden's performance, the World Cup was the big breakthrough for Holland's new variant of pressing football, which was named total football. It was also the big breakthrough for some of the biggest stars in football history, such as the Dutch Johan Cruijff, Johan Neeskens and the twins René and Willy van de Kerkhof as well as the West Germans Franz Beckenbauer, Paul Breitner, Uli Hoeness and Gerd Müller.

The final battle was between Holland and West Germany and would later be voted the best World Cup final ever played. The West Germans won, despite an early Dutch goal.

Another important meeting took place during the tournament. The draw put West and East Germany in the same group and they met in the last round of the group stage. Jürgen Sparwasser scored the only goal of the match, which made East Germany very surprisingly win the group ahead of their antagonist West Germany.

The 1974 World Cup changed football in many ways as the game was modernised. Johan Cruijff in particular was instrumental in this change and I still hold Cruijff as the best European footballer of all time - the most versatile of all. Besides, he was nice. As a coach at Barcelona in the late 1980s, he introduced total football there - something that also laid the foundation for the great success of Barcelona over the next fifteen years.

Johan Cruijff in action World Cup 1974

As I said, the 70s were fun and eventful, but also intense. In the late 70s it started to catch up with me. Like a train, which at first you hear honking far in the distance, comes closer and closer and only when it is heading straight for you do you realise that you do not have time to get out of the way.

12

Storms on All Fronts

When revolutionary things happen, you often start looking in the rear-view mirror. Looking back, it's like my path was marked out from the start. I think about how even as a child it was easy for me to socialise with all kinds of people, how I could get people to listen to me. I think back to how, as a twelve-year-old, I was able to start my own sports club. Åkeshovs IF already existed, but I wanted to start my own association so that everyone who didn't get a place at Åkeshovs IF could also play football and bandy.

I had heard from my older brothers that most of the sports associations got their money through the sale of tickets, something called the American Lottery, where the highest prize was 10,000 kroner - a huge sum at the time. In order to run a lottery, permission was required from the municipality, so I went to the municipal building and filled in a form where I wrote that the money from the lotteries would go to finance the start of the new club, IK Hjelm, which is the name I chose.

Those responsible for receiving requests of this kind were probably surprised that a twelve-year-old wanted to start a lottery. Perhaps the woman who processed my application did not take me seriously, and she informed me that I needed to have an authority figure, a police officer or the like, who could vouch for me not to take the money myself.

My brother Ernst was a policeman and it would have been easy to ask him. It's clear when I think about it in retrospect that I wanted to show that I could do it myself, without the help of my older brother. I wanted to show that I, the little boy, was just as capable as my older siblings.

Therefore, I instead went to the police station and presented my case and they answered the same as the woman at the municipality, that I needed an authority figure, and I said that was why I sought them out. The police were probably impressed by my drive and how determined I was, and they agreed, and I left with the right to start my own lottery, which allowed me to also found IK Hjelm.

It was probably the greatest moment in my career, I realise now. That's where it all started. After I had tried for several years to juggle football, the CEO job and family life, the marriage with Anna-Stina now began to break down. I had just rushed along and not really seen, or perhaps wanted to see, what was about to happen. Somewhere along the way Anna-Stina and I had started to drift apart. For me, a few tough years awaited, where a bad conscience was always present and for the first time I felt that I was not good enough.

For a long time we had lived two separate lives. I always wanted to do new things, sought new challenges and experiences, while Anna-Stina was satisfied with life at home and out on the farm. I really loved Anna-Stina and she was a fantastic mother to our daughters, but at the same time as I was climbing the career ladder, she turned into a different person.

Telling her I wanted a divorce was among the hardest things I've ever done. When I think about it today, I get that uneasy feeling back. I don't know if it can ever be easy. A divorce rarely means that both want the same thing. It is usually one who is left behind and one who bears the blame. When I told Anna-Stina how I felt and that I thought we should go our separate ways, it came as a complete shock to her. I saw a trapdoor open under her feet. Actually, we probably both felt it inside, but she probably didn't want to admit it to herself. Not that it was easy for me, but I was the one who took hold of it and was able to lean towards the meaningfulness of acting upon it.

She thought I had met someone else. I told her I had not, but it was not entirely true. During this time I had met Viola or 'Lola' as she was called. We didn't have a relationship at first, but we talked a lot and enjoyed each other's company very much. It was an eye opener for me. It was in meeting her that I realised how far Anna-Stina and I had drifted apart. It was painful.

Anna-Stina didn't believe me. After the shock came the anger. I remember how she once ran out onto the balcony and screamed that I would leave her. It was the beginning of a protracted and painful divorce that would tear open wounds in all of us. As usual, it was the children who took it the hardest. The girls took Anna-Stina's side. I understand they did it because I was the one who wanted the divorce.

Our daughter Eva came into conflict with Lola right away. I don't know exactly how it started. But unfortunately my announcement that I wanted to divorce coincided with Eva and her boyfriend Benny having started planning their wedding, which of course was not ideal. It was a chaotic time and the girls spent a lot of time supporting Anna-Stina, who completely broke down. I tried to handle it as best I could. I won't say that I escaped by working more, but it was convenient for me that I had so much to think about. During this time, I was asked to be the leader of the Swedish delegation to the World Cup in Argentina 1978. I was flattered by the offer, and it was also nice in the turbulent time in my private life to focus on work, so I accepted. It was a decision that I almost had to regret, when I was thrown into world politics.

Two years earlier, Argentine President Isabel Perón had been deposed and placed under house arrest following a military coup. In other words, the World Cup would take place in a military dictatorship, which is a rather sensitive matter. Many thought it highly inappropriate. Football became an arena for world politics, as so often happens. Many players and leaders openly criticised Argentina's leader, Jorge Videla. The Swedish national team, which had a large majority of players from Malmö FF, contained many social democrats and also leftists. MFF was a workers' club and had long been coloured by politics. Some of the national team players were also union active and well-read. Even though I was a 'Sosse' (Social Democrat), perhaps more by birth than by ideology, I avoided political discussions with the most staunch left-wing voices from Malmö FF. After a statement in the magazine *Se*, I ended up in the middle of a political storm.

I don't remember the exact quote but the gist was that I ignored politics and concentrated on football. In the national team delegation, where they wanted me to condemn Argentina's rule, this was not popular. But even though my statement made headlines in the newspaper, it ended up in the shadow of the storm that blew around the national team manager Åby Ericson.

Most people in the journalism profession at the end of the 70s were openly opposed to the World Cup going to Argentina, and both players and managers were constantly asked what they thought of the political situation in the country. There were journalists who believed that Sweden should stand up for democracy and boycott the World Cup.

When Åby was put on the spot in Buenos Aires and said that he had seen absolutely nothing of the terror with which the military junta oppressed the people, it made big, black headlines in Sweden. That a Swedish sports leader spoke so naively about the political situation was considered a great scandal. Some players in the squad thought it affected the team's performance. In addition, there were many sports journalists who thought that Åby was sitting in his position on overtime and perhaps should have given up the job to a new manager much earlier.

After the fine performance in the 1974 World Cup, Sweden was eliminated in the group stage with a shameful last place in the group. But my biggest headache was neither the national team nor politics. The divorce was a gruelling process that constantly ground me down.

It had become clear that Anna-Stina did not agree with my decision. I understood that it would take time for our daughters to accept my decision and perhaps I had thought it would be easier than it was. I moved out of our rented apartment and let Anna-Stina and our daughters stay, and I also paid for everything they needed. Anna-Stina became depressed, which gave me an even worse conscience. At the same time, I was convinced that I was doing the right thing and that in Lola I had met my soul mate.

I was used to taking action, making difficult decisions and being straightforward and honest, even when it concerned difficult things, both as CEO of Forshaga, with over 800 employees, and as chairman of AIK football. But this was something completely different, and sometimes during the long separation I felt more alone than ever. My parents had died in the mid-60s and would not have had any understanding of why I wanted to divorce if they were alive. My siblings were still here, but I didn't want to bother them with my personal conflicts. I looked up to my older brothers, perhaps mainly to Ernst. I wanted to be strong and capable, to fend for myself. It is not always a wise endeavour.

A few turbulent years awaited me, both personally and professionally. I had been chairman of AIK's main board for a long time and enjoyed it very much. Despite the fact that, as AIK's 'strong man', I had been a member of the association Swedish Elite Soccer, SEF, since 1976, I was surprised when I was asked if I could imagine becoming chairman.

The assignment differed considerably from that in AIK. As chairman of SEF, you must work for all elite clubs and not just for one. I realised what was expected of me and was once again flattered by the offer, even though I understood that I would continue to be considered an AIK member even though I would now be making everyone's case.

13

Football and Politics

1979 was a gap year: I remained in my position as chairman of AIK while I introduced the person who would succeed me. It meant a lot of stress to start my position at SEF in parallel with the CEO position at Forshaga and, in addition, a painful divorce.

Being chairman of SEF meant a new type of challenge because I had to deal with several different associations with different perspectives and agendas and there were a lot of strong characters to deal with.

> Gold you take, silver you get
> He who gapes over a little, often saves the whole
> In MFF we play in blue, but vote red

Malmö FF's legendary leader Eric Persson was a quote machine, who was also chairman of SEF for a couple of years. He was a man who did not mince words and who was initially very sceptical that SEF would be led by someone from Stockholm. He was not an easy man to get along with. The reason why I finally got his approval was actually that I was an AIK member and he respected AIK members.

Eric 'Hövdingen' Persson was both feared and infamous for his politically uncompromising stance, but at the same time highly appreciated as a straight and fair leader.

This thing about politics was sometimes very tangible and there was a lot of history and culture in the various clubs that you had to understand and take into account in order to carry out the mission. Historically, for example, all so-called peer clubs (those with the designation IFK before the club name) started in collaboration with a university.

In other words, their players came from the university, which in the Sweden of the 20s and 30s meant that it was the upper class that had the IFK star on their chest. The other clubs were so-called workers' clubs.

Being an upper-class club did not obviously mean sporting success, as the working-class clubs often had a larger catchment area to draw talent from.

An event that illustrates this happened in Malmö in 1934 when IFK Malmö, the yellow-reds, were the college boys and MFF were the workers' team. IFK reported MFF for breaching the amateur regulations, because MFF had paid out victory bonuses to the players after the SM gold, and MFF was forcibly relegated from the league. This led to a brutal rivalry between the teams.

Eric Persson's political attitude contributed to the rivalry between the teams and for him personally this meant lifelong hatred. According to some rumours, he never got into a taxi if it was yellow, and when 40 years later he saw a football match on television where one team was playing in yellow, he turned the colour off the television to avoid seeing a team playing in those colours so hateful to him.

When I took over as chairman of Swedish Elite Football, I was to turn fifty years old in the autumn, yet Eric Persson insisted at first on calling me 'our young chairman'. The task of leading the organisation into the 80s was a task that I took on with great determination.

Privately, 1979 was a difficult year, and for AIK it was also tough, as the club left the Allsvenskan for the third time in history. Some of the players who carried the team for most of the 70s did not received a new contract – among them AIK's legendary twins Yngve and Börje Leback. The legendary Gunnar Nordahl, whom I helped recruit to the club two years earlier, had been a popular coach, but unfortunately his health was failing and he suffered a heart attack, which meant that the club had to do without a coach for a while.

At the same time, match attendance figures fell throughout the season. On October 28, it was clear that AIK was joining IS Halmia down in division one and it became even gloomier when the club's great icon Putte Kock died three days later. It was a dark time and hardly the perfect handover of the presidency that I had hoped for.

The year 1979 would also be Bror Mellberg's last year on the board, but for completely different reasons from mine. For a long time we had a bingo operation that was managed by the main association with which we raised money for the team. When the accounts were prepared for the 1979 business year, we noticed that the majority of the bingo revenue was gone and we understood that something was not right. Responsibility for bingo operations had been shared between Bror Mellberg and the chairman of AIK bowling. It didn't take long before we realised that Bror Mellberg and his cronies had put large parts of the members' bingo income into their own pockets.

A furious Bruno Nyberg called Mellberg into his office and told it like it was. His cronies had already confessed so there was no point in him denying any of it. Bruno said that Mellberg's services were no longer wanted and that he could more or less go to hell.

We chose not to file a police report so that the club would avoid bad headlines in the newspapers; we simply put the lid on it. In other words, it was a bad last year as chairman of AIK, but I thought and hoped that the club would get back up to the top league right away the following year. In addition, during this time the national team was in the midst of a generational change after the World Cup fiasco in 1978.

But there was one bright spot, something that would have a big impact on Swedish football and my new role. It was when Swedish club teams began to reap success abroad. Malmö FF made it all the way to the final of the European Cup in 1979, which was a big sensation both in Sweden and abroad. The final was played in front of 68,000 people at a packed Olympia Stadion in Munich and was a much-needed triumph for Swedish football, despite them losing 1–0 to Nottingham Forest.

Many probably thought that it would be a long time before another Swedish team would repeat the feat, but on the west coast, IFK Gothenburg began to build on something that a few years later would become a golden era. Something positive had clearly been set in motion.

14

Sweden in the Football Elite

Sometimes talent can be found in the strangest and most unexpected places imaginable. Who would have thought, for example, that two brothers from the village of Palohuornas in north-eastern Lapland would become cogs in a football team from the west coast that would shock the whole of Europe during the 80s. Palohuornas, which has approximately 160 inhabitants, is located in Gällivare municipality and formerly belonged to Hakkas parish.

It was in the local association in Hakkas that the brothers Tord and Tommy Holmgren started their careers. The conditions for playing football were perhaps not quite ideal this far north in Sweden, but the brothers quickly showed that they had a talent for the game and were soon recruited to local competitor Gällivare SK.

However, they only stayed there for a year before being discovered by IFK Gothenburg in 1977. That Gothenburg had the ability to find talents for the club was widely known, but that they would recruit all the way from Lapland probably came as a shock to both supporters and the Holmgren brothers themselves.

A couple of years later, IFK Gothenburg also recruited a new coach from Degerfors. Sven-Göran 'Svennis' Eriksson had started his career as a skilled right-back in his hometown of Torsby. Via SK Sifhälla, he ended up in KB Karlskoga, where he unfortunately had to end his active career due to a knee injury. After a few years of training, he began his coaching career as an assistant to Tord Grip in Degerfors, but when he became an assistant coach for the national team, IFK Gothenburg contacted Svennis.

IFK Gothenburg had a golden generation with stars such as Torbjörn Nilsson, Glenn Hysén, Glenn Strömberg, Ruben Svensson and then the two brothers from northern Lapland – Tommy, a technically elegant midfield player, and Tord, a tough midfield dynamo. It took a few years before Svennis' plan took shape, but it would prove to bear fruit.

For me, the early 80s were intense – I was constantly getting new assignments at Swedish Elite Football, I still had the CEO job at Forshaga and the divorce was long, protracted and painful. In retrospect, it was probably my biggest defeat in life. I spent my entire professional career trying to get people to pull in the same direction, to stick together, but privately it didn't work for me at all. It hurt.

And I tried to dull the pain with more work, more responsibility. Maybe I also underestimated the consequences for my children, who were now adults, maybe I could have done it some other way, but I didn't know how. My daughters had a very hard time accepting that I had met Lola; I thought it would settle down quickly but it persisted. There were a few years when we couldn't spend time together on birthdays and other holidays. Lola used to be allowed to sit in the car while I went inside and left packages and wished Merry Christmas. At first she agreed, but not in the long run. The children probably wished that Anna-Stina and I would move in together again. When they instead found out that Lola and I had married, everything got even worse.

My daughters shut themselves off from me, while Lola's three children had no problem at all with me coming into their lives. It meant I spent more time with Lola's children than my own. The assignments for the Swedish national football team meant I had increasingly more responsibilities and there was a clear desire on the part of the association to give me even more.

In 1982 the World Cup was in Spain, and Sweden had not managed to qualify. But it was now that IFK Gothenburg would do well in the UEFA Cup. Both Malmö FF and IFK

Gothenburg participated that year, but MFF lost out during the group stage.

When IFK were to meet Valencia in the quarter-finals, many thought it was over. But it wasn't, as IFK knocked out the Spaniards after 2–0 at Gamla Ullevi. Then Kaiserslautern awaited in the semi-finals, and Sven-Göran Eriksson's IFK Gothenburg fought for important prestige in the 1–1 away match. At home, the team shocked everyone by winning 2–1 - and they were in the final against Hamburg. It was a magnificent sensation and a huge achievement for Swedish football.

After the draw, IFK would get to play at home and a whopping 42,548 came to see the first of two finals. There were many who hoped for a miracle, but still it felt like the Germans were a little too strong. The match was even and IFK held up well against the dangerous German attacks. As the game ticked past the eighty minute mark, the Germans began to slow down to play for the result, as a draw away from home gave them a huge advantage heading into the return leg in Hamburg.

Then one of the brothers from northernmost Lapland stepped into the proceedings. The tough midfielder Tord Holmgren from Palohuornas made it 1–0 in front of a jubilant home crowd and the Germans did not manage to equalise, despite a hard push in the final minutes.

When the return was played in the Volksparks Stadion in Hamburg, the pressure on the home team was enormous. There is a lot of psychology in football. Even though it only took one goal for a draw and two for a win, it's always harder to perform under pressure. Then what could not happen happened for the Germans: "The Angels" took the lead 1-0 through Dan Corneliusson. If the pressure was great before, now the Germans almost panicked. Gothenburg not only managed to keep the Germans at bay but also scored two more goals. Success was a fact.

The blue and whites (IFK) had won the UEFA Cup and suddenly all of Europe was talking about the team from Sweden that had shocked the football world. For Swedish football and for me as chairman of Swedish Elite Football, it was of course hugely gratifying.

I was called in as a representative to the Swedish Football Association's meetings more often now. The chairman of the association was Tore Brodd, a tough guy known for getting what he wanted. Unfortunately, he was perhaps even more famous for often being quite drunk, even during meetings, and whispers began behind his back that his drinking had become a problem, but no one had the strength or courage to tell him.

It happened several times when we had visits from other associations that he was not sober and it was sometimes quite embarrassing. Tore wasn't the only one in his family who had problems. His son had fallen into crime and drugs early on, which also affected Tore's well-being.

The problems escalated and finally it could not be avoided anymore – there was no other way out than for someone to confront Tore face to face. Since I was, I guess, considered a person who didn't shy away from tough situations, I was given that task.

15

Alcohol Shows No Mercy

Tore Brodd was a good person, but alcohol sometimes kills even the best, and on my way to see Tore that autumn of 1983, I couldn't help but think of another fate in the world of football. After the incredibly tragic plane crash in 1958, when almost the entire Manchester United team perished, they were forced to build a completely new team for a few years. Talent scouts travelled all over the British Isles to find young players and one day in 1963 they found an exceptional talent in Northern Ireland. The slim, dark-haired boy with the impressive ball technique was called George Best. Here began a legendary career that would unfortunately end tragically.

George Best 1976

By the age of nineteen he became one of the soccer world's superstars when, in 1966, he scored two goals against Benfica in the quarter-finals of the European Cup at the Estádio da Luz in Lisbon. The Portuguese press named Best 'the Fifth Beatle' because of his long hair, sideburns and the rock star aura he had on the pitch.

At the age of twenty-two, he had already won three of the most coveted awards: the FWA Footballer of the Year (as the youngest ever), the Ballon d'Or and the European Player of the Year award. Together with Bobby Charlton and Dennis Law, he formed what the English press called the holy trinity, which reaped success both in England and in Europe.

But there was a dark side. George Best carried a sensitivity and a darkness. The alcohol was first a way to handle the superstar status he got so quickly – too much, too soon. George quickly became a familiar face at London's most popular clubs, usually in the company of a woman and with a drink in his hand.

George Best 1982

Unfortunately, the hard life off the field caught up with him. At the beginning of the seventies, the problems began in earnest: he stopped showing up for training and was instead seen at fashionable restaurants together with beauty queen Carolyn Moore. Once he went missing for three weeks but then came back and trained with the team. The alcohol started to take its toll and he was no longer the same player.

He made his final appearance for United on New Year's Day 1974. United lost and George never turned up for training three days later. That was the last straw and George was then kicked off the team. Off the pitch, he had also been arrested during that time, on suspicion of stealing a fur coat, passport and chequebook from fashion model Marjorie Wallace.

George Best signed for new clubs over the next ten years but his escalating alcohol abuse got the better of him. Despite having to undergo a liver transplant in 2002, he could not manage to stay sober. Three years later, in October 2005, he was admitted to intensive care due to a kidney infection. Shortly afterwards, the newspapers published pictures of a sick and weak Best with skin yellowed by jaundice. George Best wanted those who read the article to see how dangerous alcohol is. In the early morning of November 25, 2005, George Best died and the cause of death was given as a lung infection and multi-organ failure.

How it would end for George Best I did not know in 1983, but even when I met him for the first time in 1967, his problems were well known. I was in London as chairman of AIK for a training tour. One morning when I was out for a walk before breakfast, as I passed a hotel, I heard someone call out "Hey Boss!" Turning, I saw the talented young goal stealer George Best outside the entrance. I went up to say hello and I remember George politely and a little shyly holding out his hand.

"George Best," he said as he introduced himself.

"I know," I said and smiled.

"I read in the newspaper that you think I'm doing well on the field and I'm grateful for that," continued George.

In connection with the visit to London, I had done a few interviews, and I had highlighted Best as the most exciting new talent.

"I just want to thank you for the nice words, because in this country the press usually writes about me in other terms," said George. "You know, I have that disease. Alcoholism. I simply can't resist the booze."

I stood there and listened as George spoke candidly about his problems. It was the beginning of a long friendship. He was always sober when we met and he was sober even then, the first time we met. He was a shy and sensitive guy with an amazing talent. He always used to dress up in a suit and tie when we met, and although I had a glass of wine with my meal, he never drank alcohol in my company.

Could anything have been done to help him? Unfortunately I don't think so. His fate rested entirely in his own hands and no matter what anyone else said or offered in advice, the inner demons came and took over.

On my way to talk to Tore Brodd, Best was on my mind. My steps felt heavy. Tore was a good person who did a lot for football. Life is sometimes very unfair, and addiction has taken many good souls. With a knot in my stomach, I reached up and rang his doorbell. My mission was to inform him that he would have no renewed confidence.

It took a while before he opened the door. His eyes were bloodshot, his hair dishevelled and his movements unsteady. Our eyes met. He stepped aside and nodded for me to enter.

"Well," said Tore, "they sent you to tell you that I'm no longer wanted."

I had expected him to be pissed off.

"You should be commended for taking on the task," he said, to my surprise. "Not many would have readily done that."

What he said next surprised me even more.

"That is why I intend to recommend you as my replacement for the post of chairman. You have shown that you have the backbone required for the job."

We sat and talked for a while. Tore was a broken man.

Tore told the media that he was going to retire and that 'his heart was in trouble'. At the same time, he took the opportunity to leave his duties at the National Sports Board. "Old men should not lead a youth movement like sports," he said, and concluded with: "Now my life will surely be a horrible existence, rootless, lonely and unbearable."

Three years later, Tore was found drowned in the bathtub in his apartment. After his death, as his successor, I had to write a few lines about him in an obituary in *Expressen* newspaper.

Tore Brodd made Sweden's name known and respected, thereby advancing our position internationally.

Perhaps less well known is the fact that Tore committed himself to his assignments with passion, and that he was tireless in the work entrusted to him, that he always looked after the little ones in the football family, that he was fearless and always careful and well-read.

Add to this that he was happy to spend a night in the circle of friends in order to be on post again early the next morning - and the picture emerges of a friendly, happy, knowledgeable and committed friend.

Now Tore is gone. The loss is great and those of us who are left behind must make sure to carry on his legacy.

Long will the memory of Tore live on.

*Visiting the international tournament for teenagers.
The tournament is named after after Lennart and the participants are the top teams in Europe.*

The Swedish King participates in the celebration of AIK (75 years old).

The trophy for winner of Swedish league. The trophy is named after Lennart and was founded in 2001.

Lennart sitting in his seat at Råsunda.

Lennart celebrating his 70th birthday at Råsunda with his granddaughter Moa.

Barbecue at summerhouse. Lennart, his brother-in-law Hubert and his friend Denis.

Crayfish with oldest daughter Eva

Eva with Lennart's mother, 1956

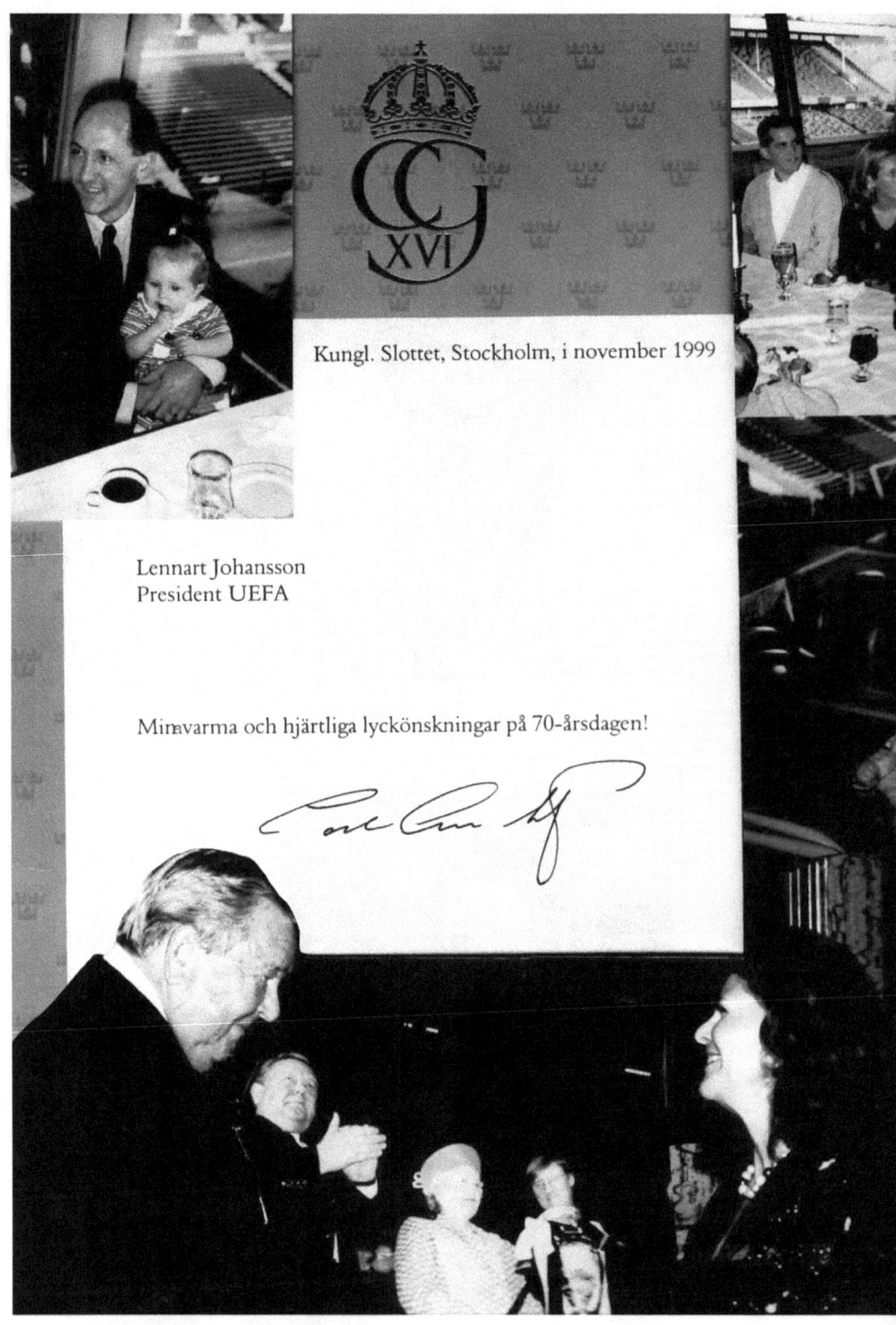

*Top right and top left: Benny and his children celebrating his 70 years birthday.
Centre: a letter from the Swedish King congratulating Lennart on his birthday.
Bottom centre: watching football at Wembley.
Bottom: Lennart and Swedish Queen, from unknown occasion.*

Lennart with his daughter Lena and Eva in Turkey.

Vacation in Switzerland

Lennart and Queen Elizabeth

Lennart and his first wife Anna-Stina in summer 1973

Sunbathing

Summer vacation at Fogdö in the archipelago

16

An Uncorrupted Role Model and a Scandal

In 1984, France was the host country for the European Championship, just as when the premiere tournament was played in 1960, and was also favourite to win gold. They had a very talented team and the one who carried Les Blues more than anyone else was midfield star Michel Platini. He was twenty-nine years old and at the height of his career. After leaving Saint-Étienne and the French league in 1982, he had really blossomed in Italian Juventus. During the European Championships at home, he formed, together with midfield colleagues Alain Giresse, Luis Fernández and Jean Tigana, a technical and extremely effective offensive which French journalists named 'carré magique', translated: magical square.

Their favourite was the European Championship, which was created by a Frenchman – and the great national hero was Michel Platini with his nine goals.

Platini was a good role model with his honest attitude. I thought, like most others, that he was one of the greatest at the time. Never in my wildest dreams could I imagine what it would be like thirty years later.

Just as Tore Brodd had told me that day when I rang his doorbell to confront him about his drinking, he had nominated me to succeed him as president of the Swedish Football Association. So I was elected chairman in 1985. In the same year, an event took place that created a lasting impression on me. It was caused by the escalating hooligan culture.

Sweden had long been spared when it came to fights and violence in connection with football matches, while England, Italy, Germany and Holland were well acquainted with the problem. That the Swedish version of hooliganism came from England was perhaps partly due to *Tipsextra*, a TV show which every Saturday broadcast matches from the English first division, but also linked to the music that was intertwined with the new hard stand culture that came from England.

The hooligan culture, which was born in the 70s, was cemented in the 80s. It was mainly during these years in the early 80s that this culture came to Sweden in earnest, initially through hockey. During the first half of the 80s, Stockholm was the capital of hockey and the Stockholm teams AIK and Djurgården took turns winning gold for a few years. AIK took the gold in 1982, Djurgården in 1983, AIK again in 1984. During these years, the rivalry grew strong and the fights in the stands between the supporters started to become a tangible problem. Football soon also saw the phenomenon of hooligan fights.

AIK's supporters' association, Black Army, took their name from Manchester United's Red Army, while arch-rivals Djurgården renamed themselves Blue Saints. Later in my career, I would regret not doing more to deal with the hooligan culture. I didn't really see at the time how much it would eat into the sport and destroy it. A supporter does his best to support his club, the hooligans do the opposite. I have a hard time understanding it.

What happened at the Heysel stadium in Brussels was a huge crowd disaster. It was 29th May 1985 when the European Cup final between Juventus and Liverpool was to be played. Even before the match there was a wave of unrest between the different clubs' supporters and the fights continued inside the arena.

The division of the supporters' seats inside the stadium was not ideal. The English had been allocated tickets in one zone, while the zone alongside was reserved for the neutral audience. But the Italians, who got hold of more tickets than the English, were also there.

It is difficult to say whether the distribution of the tickets was the triggering factor, as the English claimed, but the brawl started there in the neutral stand. Several hundred Englishmen attacked the zone and caused panic. When innocent spectators tried to escape, it was largely impossible because the escape route was blocked by a wall at the side of the stands. Shortly after the fight broke out, the wall collapsed, leading to utter chaos.

Thirty-nine people died. Of the dead, thirty-three were Italians, one French, four Belgians and one from Northern Ireland. Despite the disaster and all the dead, or perhaps because of it, angry Juventus supporters rioted in the stands and made several attempts to get over to the English. A large police operation finally put an end to the quarrel.

The disaster led to major consequences for England and English clubs in European competitions. I watched the match at home on TV, and after the scandal I was summoned as a representative of the Association to help in the talks with Liverpool.

Despite what happened, the match was played in the end, two hours late. It was a decision that felt strange after such a disaster. Juventus won the match 1–0 after the Italians were awarded a penalty. The goal scorer's name was Michel Platini.

Michel Platini playing for Juventus 1985

17

As One Star Dies, Another is Born

On the morning of March 1, 1986, I was at a conference in Karlstad, visiting Värmland's football association. Suddenly there was a knock on the door of my hotel room. When it's serious you can hear it in the small details, and I heard from the knock that it was something important. I think it was Bruno Nyberg.

"Olof Palme is dead!" he shouted.

Around Sweden, there were probably many people who woke up in a similar way as I did that morning. Prime Minister Olof Palme had been shot dead after a visit to the cinema with his wife.

I will never forget that morning. It was a great shock for the whole country. When I think back now, the feeling of shock is fresh in my mind, and I can almost see the situation in front of me. A national trauma and for me also a personal one. I met Olof Palme relatively often in various contexts and can probably say that I counted him as a friend. We used to often bump into each other on the evening flight home from Gothenburg where we had been on different missions and we made sure to end up next to each other so we could pass the time by talking football. Because he was so well versed in football, especially Swedish football, it was a real pleasure to talk to him. He was a good person and a great prime minister. It was a huge loss for Sweden. Life went on, of course, but something in Sweden had changed.

The increasingly large machinery of international football was rolling. During the spring, IFK Gothenburg managed to reach the semi-finals of the European Cup, but went out against Barcelona after penalties. It was disappointing, because IFK Gothenburg had won by a whopping 3–0 in the first match at home.

It was a shame that Sweden was not part of that summer's World Cup in Mexico. They looked good in the qualifiers, but in the final round, Portugal surprisingly beat West Germany and progressed at Sweden's expense.

In Mexico, a coming star would have his big break. The Argentinian Diego Armando Maradona had already been recognised as football's new golden boy when he left his homeland and the club Boca Juniors to seek happiness in Europe at the big club Barcelona. In the media he was called the new Pelé and Barcelona paid the then breathtaking sum of 50 million to get him to the club.

Diego Maradona 1986

Actually, Maradona was meant to be in the squad that won the home World Cup in 1978, but he was kicked out at the last moment. The fact that he didn't play that match made Maradona bitter and several times afterwards he blamed the

Argentine Football Association for taking away from him the chance to, like his predecessor and idol Pelé, become world champion already at the age of seventeen. Being kicked out also meant that Maradona decided to boycott the national team. Of course, it didn't take long before he changed his mind and in 1982 he made his World Cup debut, but the big international breakthrough came four years later in the 1986 World Cup.

With Maradona, you could also see a new type of superstar. If the likes of Beckenbauer, Cruijff and Platini often put the team first, the new breed of stars were more eccentric, with bigger egos. Maradona could sometimes talk about himself in the third person, which is now not entirely unusual among stars. For supporters and football fans, he became a watershed. You either loved him or loathed him.

Diego Maradona receiving the cup 1986

The fact that he was also surrounded early in his career by rumours of drugs and late nights in nightclubs only made his star status stronger. An entire soccer world expected the diminutive technician with the outstanding game sense to work wonders on the pitch, but few would have believed that he would bring home the World Cup title for Argentina. But that's exactly what he did - the best performance by a player in a World Cup.

The quarter-final against England would go down in history, but the feelings between Argentina and England ran much deeper than just a football match. Only four years had passed since the Falklands War, in which both Argentines and British had to give their lives in a war that from the outside seemed completely pointless. Then there was also the battle between the team's two stars. On the one hand, Maradona, who believed that even before the 1986 World Cup he was the best player the world had ever seen, and on the other hand, England's low-key but effective goalscoring king Gary Lineker, who, in addition to leading the World Cup's goalscoring league, had also taken over Maradona's place in Barcelona when the Argentine left for Italian Napoli.

Maradona showed us why he was worthy of being mentioned as one of the best in the world. Two events in the match would go down in history – the first because of Maradona, the second thanks to him.

The first: Maradona ran after the ball and although he sometimes got up high to powerfully head in a goal, this ball was way too high. Then when both England's goalkeeper Peter Shilton and Maradona jumped, it happened.

Peter Shilton was just about to put his hands around the ball when Maradona stretched out his arm and with his hand hit the ball over the goalkeeper and into the goal. Maradona did the whole motion so it looked like he was nodding. Most of the people in the arena and several of the players had seen what happened, but the referee Ali Bin Nasser awarded the goal because he himself did not see that Maradona actually used his hand. Despite cries and intense protests from the English team management, Ali Bin Nasser stood by his decision. But Maradona was not ashamed of what he had done after the match; on the contrary. After seeing the replay and also confirming himself that it was by hand, he told the assembled press that it was God's hand that made him do what he did.

The second: four minutes after God's hand, it was time for Maradona again. That time there was no doubt that it was a goal and it was also a masterpiece that has been called the goal of the century. Maradona collected the ball deep in his own half and then dribbled through pretty much the entire English team before rounding the goalkeeper and rolling the ball into the open goal.

It ended up being Maradona's major championship and he crowned the tournament as Argentina won the final against West Germany 3–2. With tears streaming down his cheeks, Maradona lifted the World Cup trophy.

Despite IFK Gothenburg's enormous success during these years, it was a really bad period for Swedish football. Gothenburg won the UEFA Cup in 1987, but the national team missed the upcoming European Championships in 1988. The championship drought continued. I and the rest of the football association's management followed IFK Gothenburg's progress in Europe and could not really understand that it was so difficult to translate that game to the national team.

The European Championship was one long revenge for a Holland that, after bitter losses in the World Cup finals of 1974 and 1978, was finally able to go all the way – this, moreover, in a European Championship with their eternal rival West Germany as host country. The EC was also the big breakthrough for a trio that would dominate European football for a few years: Frank Rijkaard, Ruud Gullit and not least - Marco van Basten.

The 80s came to an end and, to the great joy of many, so did the national team's dry spell. I remember that when it was time to celebrate my birthday on November 5th, 1989, I thought that one of the best gifts was that Sweden had finally managed to qualify for a championship again: the World Cup in Italy in 1990. Everything had gone so quickly. Already sixty years old, I found it difficult to understand and marvelled at everything I had managed to do. I still felt like the little boy who wanted to make his parents proud, who looked up to his brothers so much. But now the boy was sixty years old and chairman of the Swedish Football Association. Now Dad would see me, I thought. Then he would understand that sport was important and had taken me far. I could never have imagined this, let alone that it was just the beginning.

Quite early in my career I had promised myself never to demand special treatment. The only thing I asked for, as the trips increased and I got older, were quiet hotel rooms so I could get a good night's sleep; somthing felt increasingly important the older I got.

18

The Step up to the Top

I don't remember why, but for some reason I drove a young guy called Tomas and his father to the first meeting before the national team's training matches for the World Cup 1990. Tomas was from Hudiksvall and he had impressed in GIF Sundsvall and then came to Norrköping where he scored seven goals in nine games.

National team coach Olle Nordin had noticed the young talent and took him out to the training matches before this summer's World Cup. In the car, Tomas asked me if I thought he would be allowed to play. I replied somewhat encouragingly to the effect that he would do his best and hope to win Olle Nordin's trust. But I noticed already there in the car that this was a stubborn young man. He made it clear to me that if he wasn't allowed to play, he would go home. Besides being bold, I noticed he had a sense of humour. That Tomas Brolin would become one of our most important and popular footballers of all time, no one could have guessed back then, but in retrospect I can see that the personal qualities required to get to the top were already there.

In the midst of the most hectic preparations for the World Cup, I was faced with another challenge. Frenchman Jacques Georges announced that he did not intend to stand for re-election to the post of president of UEFA. He had held the position since 1983 and felt it was time for someone else to take over. It had long been discussed that the power in UEFA had belonged to the big soccer nations, Italy and France, ever since 1972, which made many people think that they should have a president from a smaller country. In this way, one would work to ensure that the UEFA family grew. When they suggested me, I was very surprised but of course also flattered. Apparently, my Swedish leadership style had impressed the other members of UEFA's executive committee and they believed that I had the ability to develop European football so that it benefited all member countries, not just the big ones.

I was going to turn sixty-one in the autumn, but compared to the others I was a mere lad. Moreover, I believed that I could contribute knowledge and ideas that would benefit UEFA. When I chose to accept and stand for the election, it became news that spread throughout the football world. My opponent's name was Freddy Rumo and he was chairman of the Swiss Football Association. Rumo's campaign strategy seemed to aim at smearing me, but that was not for me: I chose instead to focus on myself and what I wanted to achieve.

I knew before the election that England, Germany and France were behind my candidacy, but I was still a little surprised when I won the vote by 23–13. Thus, Sweden had received its first and so far only president of UEFA.

As it was the World Cup in 1990, it was decided that I would only take office the following year, in 1991. A special detail when I took office was that Sweden had been chosen to organise the upcoming European Championship in 1992. It was something that had already been decided and I had been saying for a long time that we were ready, but that it coincided with me becoming president was really just coincidence. The only real competitor had been Spain, but since they had already been awarded the Olympics that year, the way was open for Sweden. Unlike many others, I had been open about my intentions when I had invited representatives, for example Eastern states such as Hungary, Romania and Bulgaria, to dinners. It was obvious that I took the opportunity to present my case that Sweden could host the European Championships. You can look at dinner parties in different ways, but I was always open about what I did. I noticed that I had now entered another level of the political game. Of course, there had been intrigue and tactical play in Sweden too, but now I stepped into a world where it was serious in a completely different way. It was something I would notice, sometimes to a great extent, in an unpleasant way.

In Sweden, there were many opinions about in which cities the EC finals would take place. The Gothenburg phalanx believed that IFK Gothenburg's success in Europe qualified them as the country's football capital, while the other side believed that of course it should be in Stockholm. The biggest debate was about which city the draw would take place in, which may seem like a small thing, but the citizens of Gothenburg stood their ground. However, a leader from Gais agreed with us and said that Stockholm's city hall with the three crowns is perhaps one of Sweden's most symbolic buildings. In the end, all parties were satisfied and it was fair, as the draw and inauguration took place in Stockholm but the final itself took place at Nya Ullevi in Gothenburg.

But first there was the World Cup, and I was to take office the following year, when I had had some time to digest that I would soon be president of UEFA.

Expectations for the Swedish national team ahead of the World Cup in Italy 1990 were high, not only due to good efforts during the qualifiers, but also because Sweden was drawn in a relatively easy group. In addition, the Swedish people had longed to see Sweden in a championship again after a difficult 1980s when the national team failed to qualify for all tournaments.

But Sweden flopped despite the high expectations and never progressed from the group stage. The disappointment at home in Sweden was great after the tournament and coach Olle Nordin made his place available. A disappointed Glenn Hysén summed up his feelings like this: "This was a dick... Now you get to be a brilliant at midsummer."

There were probably more than Glenn Hysén who became brilliant on Midsummer Eve 1990.

The final was between West Germany and Argentina, and the Germans got revenge for the final loss four years earlier. It was an uneventful match and Andreas Brehme scored the only goal, a penalty, at the end. The Germans could raise their bows to the sky and dance in a ring while Maradona stood in the background with tears streaming down his cheeks. A few years later I would play a role in what would be the end point of Maradona's career. But of course, I had no idea at the time. Despite the final loss, Maradona was still the greatest, and his stardom was huge, more than he could handle.

Far away from the world's attention and the glamour enjoyed by men's football, an intense campaign was underway for women's football to have an official World Cup tournament as well. I am proud that I pursued this issue during this time and that Sweden was at the forefront when it came to women's football. In the end, it all worked out and the first official Women's World Cup was to be held in China the following year. It was very gratifying.

But for me, everything that happened after the World Cup in Italy was about preparing myself to shoulder the presidency of UEFA, and now the preparations for the European Championships on home soil started. It would be a flying start at the new job, to say the least.

19

The Shot

We sat at the Grand Hôtel and had dinner with the presidents of the participating nations and their respective wives. It was a really nice evening; we talked about the tournament, various arrangements and events connected to it. But there had been a dramatic turn of events in the last few weeks and days that cast a shadow over the dinner. In Yugoslavia, full civil war had broken out in several parts of the country. Participating in the European Championship in 1992 was out of the question, but Yugoslavia's national team had managed to get to Sweden already and were at a training camp up in Dalarna. Yugoslavia was also counted as one of Europe's best national teams with many big players.

I had received a call from UN Secretary General Kofi Annan who announced that Yugoslavia would not be allowed to participate in any international competitions. So the decision was the UN's, but they left it to UEFA to announce it. In retrospect, it might seem a little strange. I had no opportunity to influence the decision, and what made the situation even worse was that the Yugoslav national team was already there. I announced the decision, which of course was not fun. The Yugoslavs were incredibly disappointed and angry. When we sat there at dinner at the Grand Hôtel, a few days had passed since they left Sweden.

When Yugoslavia was excluded, we had to fill their place. The country that was lucky, due to the results in the qualifiers, was Denmark, which would turn out to result in the Danes' greatest football success ever. It was thus an intense start to my presidency.

The Danes were of course overjoyed, while the Yugoslavs responded with anger from the team, the federation and from the political side.

When it was time to round off the dinner at the Grand Hôtel, Lola and I jumped into a taxi to go out to our villa in Södra Ängby. Most of the other dinner guests stayed at the hotel. Just before we could get into the waiting taxi, a black car pulled up alongside us and rolled down the side window. I turned to face the car, which had slowed down.

"We're going to kill you, you fat bastard," said a man with a strong accent. I had time to see the window go up again before it picked up speed.

For a few seconds I stood looking away along the road after the car sped off.

"Lennart, Lennart..!" I heard Lola's voice. She was absolutely terrified. My mind was spinning. I assumed the threat was because of Yugoslavia's exclusion. Lola's hand held mine during the car ride home. What happened felt serious - this was no ordinary upset supporter who drove by. This was serious.

A few days later, we were in bed sleeping in our house in Södra Ängby when we both woke up with a jolt. There was a sound. It clattered - bangs, close together. For a second we were both as confused as you are when you've just woken up and find yourself in some kind of borderland. Then came the panic. Gunfire - my God, someone is shooting!

We got up. Lola shouted something that I didn't catch. I threw myself at the phone and dialled the emergency number. We heard glass shattering. Lola cried and shook. The seconds felt like eternities. I don't remember what I said to the operator who answered, I probably screamed at them.

When the police arrived, they could immediately ascertain that someone had driven past and fired with an automatic weapon at the house and that several bullets had punched holes in the facade, broken several windows and shot down some roof tiles. About ten shots had been fired.

I paced anxiously up and down the house with a big lump in my stomach. Säpo (Swedish Special Police) came the same day and informed us that from now on we would have police protection around the clock. The incident was never leaked to the media. The police and Säpo were careful that it would be handled completely confidentially as it could create panic and chaos if it came out that the UEFA president had been shot at in his own home in the middle of the European Championship.

Who the perpetrators were never came out, but of course I understood that it had to do with Yugoslavia's exclusion. Both Lola and I had to sign confidentiality papers, in which we promised not to speak about the incident, something I think the nearest neighbours also had to do. After the shots, there were police in our garden around the clock.

I also remember an occasion when I was driving towards Norrköping and noticed that someone was following me. It was not funny. I was blamed for a decision made by the United Nations.

Only six years had passed since Olof Palme was shot on Sveavägen and I noticed that the police took this very seriously. For a few months we had to live with police surveillance. In the kitchen, in the garden, in the basement and the garage. Every time I went somewhere, bodyguards came with me.

The war escalated in Yugoslavia. There were enormously strong emotions. I remember that I was going to take a taxi on one occasion during the tournament, but I had to change cars when the driver saw that it was me, because he was a Serb.

Only those closest to me knew what had happened. I tried to keep a up good facade, and I didn't want it to affect me; I didn't want them to win in any way by throwing me off balance. It was true, to say the least, that I was thrown straight into the hot seat at the beginning of my presidency.

While I lived with a threat hanging over me, Tomas Brolin and the national team impressed on the pitch. Perhaps the Yugoslavs' hatred of UEFA was also strengthened by the fact that their replacement, Denmark, did very well. Sweden surprisingly won their group against France and then won against both England and Denmark.

This meant that Sweden and Denmark advanced to the semi-finals and not England and France as expected. In 1992, coach Tommy Svensson had brought through a new generation that seemed to get along very well together. In the national team, I thought I saw a joy and solidarity within the group. It filled me with confidence. Just before the tournament I had spoken to Tommy and given him a note with ten points that I consider important for winning. The points on the note were really quite self-explanatory, but I was convinced that Tommy would understand that what I meant was if you could get a whole group to strive for these, it would create community and a great strength. This led to several conversations based on them, and Tommy then summarised the conclusions in a couple of points with shorter explanations. He then gathered the national team squad and went through what he had written, and handed out a paper to the players that read:

Play with your heart!
Everyone has the right to make mistakes, but no one has the right not to give 100% effort.

Think positively!
Positive thoughts produce positive results. See the possibilities, not the problems!

Show courage - dare!
Don't pass the responsibility on to someone else.
Dare to use what you are good at!

Think that you are good with others!
Try to make your fellow players good!

A strong will can overcome most things!
Motivation beats class! Create an inner desire for success!

Speak a winning language!
"I can, I want, I dare, I will!"

Show engagement!
Joy, enthusiasm... body language!

Own responsibility for the best of the team!
Team spirit - winning spirit!

Now I don't know if my points helped, but he had assembled a team. And Sweden thus won their group. In the second group, however, there were no surprises when Germany and Holland went ahead and knocked out Russia, which then went by the name CIS, the Commonwealth of Independent States, and Scotland.

Sweden went out against Germany in the semi-final, which was then pitted against the sensational Denmark, who had shocked everyone by making it all the way. In the final, the Danes also took the lead a bit into the first half. The Germans pressed hard. They shot, passed and lifted balls far into the penalty area, but Denmark held tight. Opportunities opened up for counterattacks and that's exactly what happened in the 78th minute when Kim Vilfort shot from distance, a not-too-hard shot that caught the inside of the post before rolling over the goal line. After that, the air went out of the Germans and Denmark won the entire tournament, taking the country's only Championship medal to date.

The European Cup in Sweden was not only a victory for Denmark, but also for football at home. Sweden had something going on and Denmark's win had shown that it is possible to bring down even the big giants if you have a good day. Even for me, the Championship was a great success despite the unpleasantness that happened before it.

Shortly after the end of the European Cup finals, I needed to go on a business trip for Forshaga to Zagreb in what is today Croatia but was then in Yugoslavia. When I got on the plane, the flight attendant said: "Do you dare to go now?" At first I was scared and thought that it might not be appropriate to go to Yugoslavia. But then the flight attendant told me that it had appeared in the Yugoslav media that I was not at fault for the exclusion. Then I could exhale a sigh of relief.

After the successful European Championship in Sweden, Tommy Svensson continued to build on a core of players that he succeeded in turning into an incredibly close-knit group before the World Cup in the USA in 1994.

20

The Tournament of Champions

For me, 1992 was one of the most successful years of my career. The idea that would change everything had already hit me after the World Cup two years earlier. I had begun to think about whether it was possible to create an attractive tournament for European club football, something similar to the power of a World Cup. The European Cup was not something the clubs found particularly prestigious and the media's interest was lukewarm. UEFA had for a long time been dragged along with lousy finances, which in the long run would be bad for the development of European football.

Immediately upon taking office as president, I realised the extent of the poor economy that would form the basis of our operations. My good friend and UEFA general secretary Gerhard Aigner was of the same opinion. After many long discussions between the two of us, the idea crystallised to replace the European Cup with the Champions League and create a more modern tournament, where double meetings became group games and where UEFA would negotiate television agreements and take care of the negotiations with sponsors. We immediately met strong opposition from FIFA and Sepp Blatter, who feared that UEFA would eventually become bigger than FIFA as a result of this. Since the first time I met Blatter, I felt a great discomfort with him as a person. A discomfort that would be confirmed several times over.

The fact that I was the newly appointed president and rather quickly started with such plans probably stung a little extra in Blatter's eyes. Our ideas were seen as a threat to FIFA , which for a long time was football's absolute heavyweight and most powerful organisation. Great nations like England were hesitant.

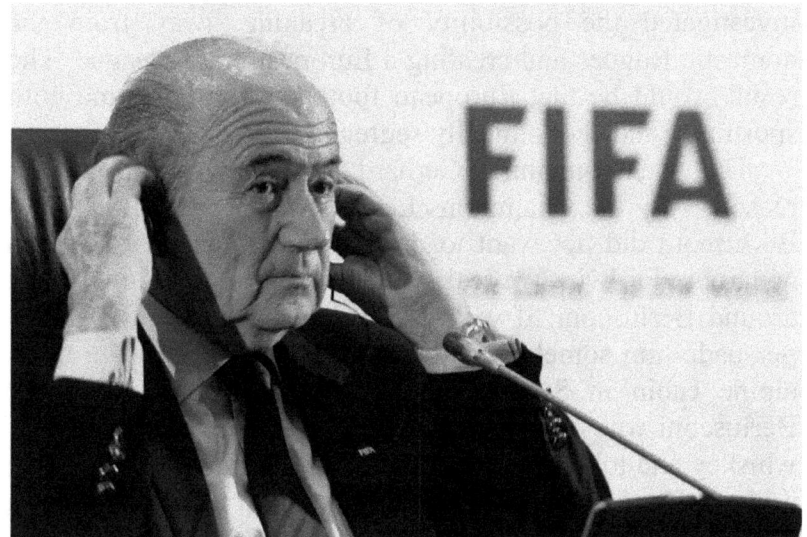

Sepp Blatter

Gerhard Aigner and I were now faced with the task of making strong financial connections to the project with the Champions League and after probing the market we noticed that there seemed to be some interest. Some teams were directly linked to big companies through sponsorship and sometimes even the government itself was involved and sponsored. In Spain, it has long been known that the government was behind Real Madrid, which makes the club both special and perhaps even unsporting in comparison to Spain's other clubs. Also, one of the clubs that belonged to Europe's top tier in the late 80s and early 90s was Milan.

When it comes to Italian clubs, ownership is often even tighter than other countries' club teams. Silvio Berlusconi was one of the fiercest opponents of our idea. He was not just anyone but one of the most powerful men in European football at this time. He not only owned Milan but also the country's largest television and radio channels and a couple of years later he also became prime minister of Italy. In addition, he was one of the founders of what would later be known as the G-14. For a few years, Europe's fourteen biggest clubs investigated the possibility of breaking away from the domestic leagues and creating a European major league. The result would be that European football would become both sportingly and economically segregated.

That was something Gerhard and I saw as one of the reasons why the Champions League was needed. But Silvio Berlusconi did not want to drop a tournament that his own Milan used to win. We realised that we were not going to get around Berlusconi; if we were to have a chance we had to persuade him somehow. I therefore invited Berlusconi to an alpine cabin in Switzerland. It was in the afternoon but Berlusconi was hungover and tired. I offered him a glass of whiskey and told him that as the owner of a big club and also a big media company, he could make a lot of money from a tournament like the Champions League. After a couple of hours he suddenly said:

"Okay, we're driving."

The meeting with Berlusconi was the key that made the rest fall into place. After our meeting, he became a strong advocate for the tournament and he persuaded several other big clubs. One change I saw as necessary was that UEFA as an organisation would get closer to the clubs and their operations. For a long time, communication with the member clubs had been very formal, which meant that the clubs might not always believe that UEFA was doing everything in their best interest.

I thought it would be good to have a person whose task it was to keep in touch with the clubs on a regular basis, to inform them about changes and perhaps above all to listen to the clubs' own opinions. That's why I hired Scotland's former national team coach Andy Roxburgh, who in his capacity as Technical Director came to function as UEFA's extended arm.

In addition to anchoring with the clubs, commercial muscle was required. Gerhard and I understood quite quickly that we needed someone from the outside who could drive the marketing of the tournament to a different level than we could handle ourselves.

It was two Swiss businessmen, Klaus Hempel and Jürgen Lenz, who took on the task of commercialising the Champions League to the level we wanted it to be. They did a fantastic job and it wasn't long before the big companies were queuing up to participate and be seen in connection with the tournament.

It became more and more clear that the Champions League would be a success, but we could not have imagined that it would reach the breadth and turnover it has today. At first, we were most satisfied that we had saved UEFA from its bad financial situation. Now it has almost become too big, with too much money - I am actually not convinced that it is entirely positive. Our thought, perhaps somewhat naively, was that the Champions League would broaden football and give the clubs of small nations a greater chance to show off on the bigger stage. Today, instead, it can be argued that there are generally only seven or eight clubs that have a chance of winning the tournament. And the cash flow turned out to be enormous.

When the first Champions League final kicked off in 1993 at the Olympic Stadium in Munich, French Marseille faced Italian Milan. Silvio Berlusconi and other Milan supporters were fully prepared for the trophy to end up in Milan, but Marseille wanted otherwise. The French had for a few years built a strong team with, among others, the English star Chris Waddle and the shooting king Jean-Pierre Papin.

At the end of the first half, Basile Boli scored the goal that would see Marseille become the first French team ever to win Europe's biggest club title.

Unfortunately, the French triumph was overshadowed, as Marseille's club director Bernard Tapie was revealed to be involved in a major bribery scandal, causing the club to face a few tough years. Milan shook off the loss and were back in the final the very next year, against a Barcelona led by coach Johan Cruijff and with a young Pep Guardiola as defensive midfielder. However, Barcelona's defence collapsed and Milan were able to easily win 4–0, much to Berlusconi's delight.

Every year, for fifteen years, I was the prize-giver after the Champions League final. I am extremely proud to have created one of the world's biggest tournaments. Only one thing in my career hits higher, and that is when I founded the association IK Hjelm on my own. It trumps the Champions League.

21

Success and Falling Stars

Most things worked out for Sweden. Tommy Svensson had really put together a team for the World Cup finals in the USA in 1994. I had been appointed the highest manager over the entire World Cup and I would not have to be ashamed of my countrymen. There was something special about the atmosphere that summer and the crowd and the team were in harmony. We had football fever.

The matches were often played late in the evening or in the middle of the night, Swedish time. There were probably many sleepy Swedes who set the clock to two in the morning to watch Sweden's opening match against Cameroon. At first it looked good as Sweden took the lead, but after two quick goals by Cameroon, the pattern from 1990 looked to be repeating itself. The one who broke this pattern was a young talent from Helsingborg who, with swaying braids, made a shot into the crossbar that Martin Dahlin was then able to put into the goal so that the match ended 2–2. Not a perfect result against an on-paper worse opponent, but still a good start to the tournament.

As the midsummer weekend approached in Sweden, heavy rain clouds were in the air and many disappointedly thought that it would be another rainy midsummer. But then the miracle happened: around lunchtime on Midsummer Eve, the sun broke through the clouds and all the tables set indoors were taken out to the garden again. A high pressure area moved in over Sweden that would last for a while into August.

Sweden's next match, against Russia, was played around midnight Swedish time. After some persuasion, Tommy

Svensson had changed the lineup so that Tomas Brolin played as a midfielder behind the strikers Kennet Andersson and Martin Dahlin. It was a change that would prove to be a stroke of genius.

Many midsummer-celebrating Swedes probably shouted their disappointment when Russia was awarded a penalty after just four minutes. Penalty shooter Salenko showed no nerves and 0–1 was a fact. But before the first half was over, the referee had time to blow for another penalty, this time for Sweden. Tomas Brolin did not want to be worse than Salenko and at half time it was 1-1.

In the second half, Sweden came out like a completely new team and really upped the tempo, and in the 59th minute it was time for Martin Dahlin to get on the scoresheet when he made it 2-1. The Russians tried to come back and pressure Sweden, which opened up counter-attacks - often led by Tomas Brolin.

One of those runs ended with Brolin hitting a cross that was met by a leaping header from Martin Dahlin, and there were cheers on the Swedish midsummer night.

In the final group stage match, Sweden's acquaintance Brazil awaited them, who, via two victories, were already through to the next round.

That Tommy Svensson really got something special out of this team was already clear because the win against Russia meant that we progressed; but could we surprise against Brazil as well? Brazil had their superstars in Romário and Bebeto. Sweden, on the other hand, had a striker who had yet to score a goal in the tournament. The lanky Sörmlander Kennet Andersson, raised in IFK Eskilstuna, took the chance when everyone least expected it.

In an attack where Kennet received the ball in a position that usually does not result in a scoring opportunity, he surprised everyone, including Brazil's goalkeeper, when he lifted the ball into the far end of the goal with an outside side kick. His goal celebration, with the index fingers like pistols, came to be as classic as Orup, Glenmark and Strömstedt's World Cup song 'När vi gräver guld i USA' ('When we dig for gold in the USA'). The fact that Romário equalised at the beginning of the second half did not mean much. Sweden was still ahead.

I obviously followed Sweden's progress in the competition, but my main focus was on something else. For four years I had been president of UEFA and was appointed as the so-called 'supreme manager' during the World Cup. I was also part of the group that, together with WADA, the anti-doping association, would work for a clean tournament.

For Maradona, the talk since the 1990 World Cup had mostly been about suspected drug problems and trouble with the law. He had been counted out as a player by most people when the news came that he was in the Argentine squad.

There were problems with that squad right away. We had agreed on some rules for the active players, which included certain times in the evening when players and leaders would be at their hotel. A curfew. The rules were there to avoid possible scandals with players and managers on late night club visits. The first to break the rules were Argentina. They especially had a hard time staying within the time frames, I remember. They claimed that it was difficult to acclimatise to the time change in another time zone, which was, of course, nonsense.

Maradona was one of the players who consistently ignored all the rules, even when it came to appearing for the doping controls.

During this time, his drastic weight loss had fuelled persistent rumours of possible drug abuse, which was not surprising since he had been busted several times for cocaine possession in Argentina. When Argentina then played their first game in the tournament, all eyes were once again on the little technical wizard from Buenos Aires. Everyone thought he was counted out, but when he punched in his first goal, the whole arena exploded. Maradona ran out to the cameraman behind the goal and stared madly into the camera while pointing to the Argentine national emblem on his chest.

Argentina won over Greece 4–0 and the soon-to-be thirty-four-year-old Maradona made a big impression. The success also continued in the next match against Nigeria, where Argentina won 2–1 after two goals by Claudio Caniggia. Everything looked good and Argentina with Maradona were already set for the round of 16 and well on their way to winning the group.

After the match, a large gathering of press was waiting for Maradona to come out and, in his typical way, smile superiorly while he talked about how it would happen and when Maradona would make Argentina world champions again. But there was no Maradona.

For two hours the press waited and from the players who came out you could tell that something was not right. The Argentine players who had just won went out with their eyes downcast and hurried past the journalists and into the waiting bus. That's not how a team that just won and was on its way to success behaves.

When the bus then drove towards the hotel without Maradona getting out, everyone understood what had happened. The Argentine superstar had been caught in the doping control and tested positive for ephedrine. The scandal broke and all the world's sports pages were filled with the story of how Maradona had been caught doped and had played his last game for Argentina. FIFA president João Havelange tried to hush up the scandal, but it was too late.

I was there when Maradona was caught and I was happy to be able to show the world that cheating and doping do not belong in a world championship. I guess after what happened, Maradona didn't think too highly of me, but I didn't care.

Despite the suspension, Maradona used to appear in the stands at Champions League finals and the World Cup, often smoking a cigar and gossiping, and you could tell by the change in his body that he was living an unhealthy lifestyle. As a player he was fantastic and one of the best ever, but as a person he was problematic, a cheat who seemed mostly interested in cultivating attention for himself.

The Argentinian squad was affected by what happened, losing the final group stage match against Bulgaria 2–0 and finishing second in the group, which meant they faced slightly more difficult opposition in the round of 16 in the form of Romania.

In retrospect, World Cup 1994 is seen as the championship that in many ways saved football in Sweden, both as a popular movement and as an attraction. The Swedish national league football felt lukewarm and the interest in ice hockey's elite series was significantly greater. After the World Cup, the temperature in the Allsvenskan increased considerably.

And there was nothing wrong with the temperature that summer either – it was similar to the heat on the sunny Spanish coast. Feverishly, we began to dream of a new 1958. Many who sat in front of the television sets saw the close-knit gang that Tommy Svensson had put together. A different approach, which was met with scepticism and astonishment among the journalists, was when it emerged that Tommy Svensson read a poem by Karin Boye to the players before the round of 16 match against Saudi Arabia. It was a comfortable 3–1 victory for the Swedes.

In the quarter-finals, the next opponent awaited, Romania, who after an entertaining match had knocked out Argentina. The Romanians, like the Swedes, had managed to be on top form with a golden generation of great players such as Hagi, Dumitrescu and Popescu.

The match against Romania would come to symbolise the entire magical World Cup summer with hope and despair and a drama that felt close to unbearable for the viewers who sat there and sweated on the TV sofas. Sweden scored first through an ingenious free-kick variation where Mild passed to Brolin, who thundered the ball into the goal. Romania equalised, and then it was into extra time, where the Romanians seemed to have decided the match with their second goal. And then Kennet Andersson's header, as he eased off the ground, higher than the Romanian goalkeeper, took the game to penalties. Thomas Ravelli's decisive save in the shootout is the very image of Tommy Svensson's national team. A national team that never seemed to give up.

Tommy Svensson and the Swedish football team arrive back in Sweden July 18th 1994 after the World Cup

Maybe Sweden could have reached the final. Some have subsequently wondered and speculated whether some strange decisions were not made both before and during the semi-final against Brazil.

When it became clear that Sweden would face Brazil in the semi-finals, they knew roughly what kind of opposition it was because they had played to a draw against them in the group stage.

The first strange thing that happened was that the referee who was announced to officiate the match was replaced the day before, without any explanation whatsoever. Instead of the European referee that was intended, it became a Colombian referee. When then Jonas Thern received a red card and was sent off after a melee with Brazil's hard-driving Dunga, some began to feel uneasy.

In the stands sat the Brazilian FIFA boss Havelange. And considering what would come to light later, it may not be entirely improbable that he had a hand in the game.

In any case, it was bronze for Sweden after a proper thrashing of Bulgaria with 4–0. Kennet Andersson scored a total of five goals in the tournament and Brolin was selected for the WC's world team. Brazil won the final against Italy on penalties.

Several Swedish coaches and players were successful abroad, such as Svennis, Tord Grip and Henke Larsson. The man in the stands who watched Sweden's match against Brazil, the FIFA president, João Havelange, I would have to deal with later, when I gradually approached the wasps' nest. Something definitely smelled…

22

Into the Lion's Den

Had I known how dirty the power play behind the scenes was, I might not have run for office. During my years in international football, I had of course heard a lot of talk about corruption and bribery. Maybe I was a little naive, but I had a genuine hope to try to make the sport more clean and honest. I wanted to try. Havelange had announced that he intended to resign and a new president would be appointed. I had decided that I would run for office.

In the autumn I would turn sixty-nine years old, an age when many others start thinking about retirement - but not me. Before that, there would be a World Cup in France where I would once again be the top manager. The election for the post of FIFA president was to be held just before the start of the World Cup in June 1998.

I was not alone in wanting to become president – Sepp Blatter, who had been FIFA's general secretary since 1981, also wanted the post. While my career until now had mainly consisted of coincidences, the candidacy for FIFA was the first time that I actively sought a position.

With hindsight, it is easy to see that it was Sepp Blatter who was my absolute biggest opponent, a competitor for the soul of football.

The two of us have completely different backgrounds. I come from humble circumstances while the Swiss Sepp Blatter comes from a wealthy family. He trained in economics and law and made a fortune in the watch industry before venturing into the world of sports. Sepp Blatter's first big assignment was as general secretary of the Swiss Ice Hockey Association.

Through contacts in both the sports and business worlds, he came to be part of the organisation around the 1972 and 1976 Olympics. As early as 1975, Sepp was named technical director at FIFA and shortly afterwards he rose to the position of general secretary. The then FIFA president João Havelange was early surrounded by rumours of corruption and bribery; already in 1992 the Dutch newspaper *De Telegraaf* reported that Havelange had accepted bribes in the form of gifts, diamonds and art in connection with Amsterdam's bid for the 1992 Summer Olympics.

Peter Kronenberg, who was press manager for Amsterdam's application, then testified that Havelange had 'very special wishes' for him to put in a good word for their application. When there were more accusations of bribery and corruption, Havelange suddenly announced that he did not intend to stand for re-election as FIFA president, after twenty-four years in the post. Sepp Blatter was close friends with Havelange. I had no easy opponent.

But I wasn't without friends. Some who would support my candidacy were the superstar Pelé and the German star Franz Beckenbauer. As UEFA had grown into a larger organisation under my leadership, I hoped for voices from many of the smaller countries that I had helped to become part of the great European football family.

In addition, I held the post of vice-chairman of FIFA and there is usually a normal order of succession. As vice-chairman of FIFA , I had worked hard to ensure that African football would receive more attention and receive the same professional organisation as European football. I was very good friends with the president of the African Football Federation, Issa Hayatou from Cameroon, and together with him had started several collaborations that would benefit both club teams and national teams in Africa.

I thought that, above all, I had strong credentials in what I accomplished. Of course, I had my suspicions about how the friendship between Sepp Blatter and outgoing chairman

Havelange could influence the vote. But still, I had to believe I could win.

Sepp Blatter had of course also hired famous names to campaign for him and the most active was a man called Jack Warner, who represented the small country of Trinidad and Tobago in the West Indies. The election would of course be held in Zurich, where FIFA has its headquarters and where both Sepp Blatter and Havelange lived.

With me to Zurich came my youngest daughter, Lena. She was the one of my daughters who quickly got over the divorce and accepted Lola. You could feel the rivalry at the election, you could feel it in the air. Lena later said that she immediately saw that something was wrong. Sepp Blatter and his entourage were busy greeting all the delegates from Africa and Asia.

Smiles, fake laughs and nervous back pounding was happening. Welcome gifts were handed out and an Arab prince who no one really knew came in and gave Sepp Blatter a kiss on the cheek. I had a more reserved style and sat with my delegation and waited for the results of the vote. I looked around at the looks that were exchanged - but perhaps above all at the looks that turned away. Something was in the making.

Just before Havelange resigned, he announced that he was behind a World Cup in England, to the delight of Tony Blair. Tony Blair and the English organisation had clearly announced that they would like to see me as the new president of FIFA . Havelange, on the other hand, preferred to highlight Sepp Blatter as his candidate. However, I was the favourite because the Germans and the English had a gentlemen's agreement which meant that they would not vote against each other on the issue. Basically, it was about Germany supporting England's application for the European Championship in 1996 and the English application for the World Cup in 2006. But Havelange managed to break that agreement and instead announced an election between me and Blatter. That the Swiss was secretary general and running for president was not appropriate. At a meeting with the executive committee of

FIFA, I had demanded that Sepp Blatter resign as general secretary if he had thoughts of becoming president. Havelange rejected my demand and ended the meeting before members had a chance to vote on it. Personally, I thought that a lavish election campaign to get the presidency was nonsense and believed that the money should instead be spent on football itself.

It was crowded in the room and I will never forget one incident - then I really felt that something was wrong. My good friend Issa Hayatou from Cameroon came up to me. There was something about him, something he didn't say with words but with his body language. He greeted me and I remember there was something in his eyes, he was sad, maybe ashamed. The eyes don't lie.

"Don't you realise that you are being deceived. They bribe people right in front of our eyes," Lena told me. If it was so, it would show, I thought. I didn't want to make a scene if I didn't win, because it could be interpreted as me being a bad loser. But then it came, the result.

Sepp Blatter won the vote with 111 votes to my 80. Immediately voices were raised about bribery and corruption. What actually happened, who paid whom and who was behind the election of the next FIFA president has never really been made clear.

I showed no feelings then and there. I made an effort to keep it inside. But the disappointment was huge. I felt betrayed. I understood that the African states that had showed me their support during the campaign had been bought to vote for Sepp Blatter.

I sensed that wasn't the end of the story. But I was responsible for the World Cup that was soon to be played in France: duty called and made me think of other things.

23

Catching My Breath at Vätö

I looked out the window and let my gaze drift over the water. I filled my chest with air and then exhaled slowly. I felt at home here. I had completed my mission during the World Cup and I then went to our summer house on the island of Vätö. It had been a tough year so far. For the first time, I had been personally exposed to the way money can buy power in top international football.

The World Cup in France had been a good championship with a great audience. My mood was clouded after the sloppy election just before the World Cup; I was disappointed and harbouring anger and resentment. I tried to avoid sports, which throughout my life had given me such enormous comfort and inspiration.

The World Cup was a great triumph for the host nation, France. They had a fantastic team led by Zinedine Zidane and also a very good home crowd that was thirsty for a title. It turned out to be a success story: in the final, the most influential players of the tournament met, Ronaldo from Brazil and Zidane from France. It was set up for a super tight game, but it was an easy victory for France after two headers from Zidane and a third from Petit.

After the victory, the huge Champs-Élysées was filled with triumphant Frenchmen, the Arc de Triomphe drawing its silhouette against the sky in celebration of the nation's first title. It is for them – for the people – that football is for, they are the ones we should work for, I thought.

But it was difficult to let go of what had had happened. That Havelange, Blatter and their gang had bribed people for themselves to win the vote was beyond doubt for me. At home in Sweden, I had done a few interviews where I expressed my dissatisfaction with the election and what had happened.

As soon as I got a little quiet time, I had gone to Vätö to think and let everything sink in. The most painful thing during the World Cup was how, during the opening ceremony, I had to shake hands with several representatives from countries that Blatter had bribed and who now stood there complaining that I had lost the vote. The fake smiles and backstabbing of corruption was hard for me to digest, it goes against everything I believe in. It pissed me off.

1998 was in many ways a very hard year, but at the end something came that lightened everything up. It was that my beloved AIK won gold, which was also the start of a very eventful period for the Rats. The following year, a large investment was made in the Champions League and AIK made it to the group stage and had to face Barcelona, Arsenal and Fiorentina. It was quite clear that AIK would find it difficult to progress from the group. The club, on the other hand, would make a lot of money from ticket revenue. The team did well, and one of the most memorable performances was against Barcelona at home.

Above all, Nebojsa Novakovic's goal when he lobbed the ball over the goalkeeper is classed as one of the club's most historic. Nebo, as he is called, came to Sweden from wartime Yugoslavia. As a child he played football in the streets of Sarajevo but his hometown was destroyed in the war and the family was forced to flee. Nebo's history from street football to a dream goal in the Champions League sums up the game and in many ways also the strength of sport. At the Sports Gala that year, I had the honour of presenting the goal of the year award to Nebosja. That gave me strength during periods of adversity. Football is like life: hits and misses. I was present during the Champions League final the following year between Bayern Munich and Manchester United, which was played in Barcelona. It would be one of the most dramatic finals ever. Next to me in the VIP stand sat my closest friend, Gerhard Aigner, who was the general secretary of UEFA. With only a few minutes left in the game, we got up to collect the trophy and medals. Bayern Munich led the match 1–0 on this occasion. We took the lift down through the arena, where I met Bobby Charlton and we lamented the loss. When we got onto the pitch, I went straight up to Karl-Heinz Rummenigge, who was the chairman of Bayern Munich, to congratulate him.

"The trophy goes to Manchester United," he told me.

He must have seen on my face that I didn't understand, as I stood wondering if he was joking.

"We conceded two goals in the last ninety seconds," he clarified, and then I realised he was serious.

"Such is life. That's how football is," I said then and put my arm around him.

24

Money Money Money

That AIK followed the trend at the turn of the millennium and was incorporated was not something that I was overly positive about. I was brought up in association life and was CEO of a large company, so I understood what difficulties could arise when an association and a company were to merge. There are two different ways of conducting business. In an association, you really work from the bottom up, democratically and long-term. The business world is more about short-term profits.

This was also when the problems started. People quickly appeared in the club with completely different interests from those who had run the business before. During the period 2000–2003, AIK Fotboll AB lost almost SEK 40 million. The shares basically became worthless.

I was elected chairman of the board even though it was not something I wanted myself, but it was about standing up and taking responsibility and trying to clean up the finances to save the licence.

But it was not easy for me to have full control of AIK when I had my duties for UEFA at the same time. Unfortunately, I think that the corporatisation made us a bit blind to the speed of things, which usually doesn't pay off in the long run.

It was not only AIK that was corporatised during these years: it was a wind that blew across the country and the sports supplements sometimes felt like business magazines. At the same time as Swedish elite football underwent a major change, Stockholm also took over the place as the country's leading football city.

Gothenburg had for a long time had great success both in the Swedish league and internationally - with four straight SC golds in 1993–1996 - but after AIK's gold in 1998, it was the Stockholm team that came to dominate, also in terms of audiences.

Despite that, AIK's shine since the golden year and the Champions League had fallen somewhat and instead of trying to get stability in the club, coaches were replaced like on an assembly line. It was a turbulent time in AIK Football's history. In 2002, AIK managed the feat of using three coaches in one season. There were many who seemed to forget how important continuity is in football. The club changed a lot and division was sown instead of community.

I can't say that I had full insight into the decisions that were made about the sporting part because I was so busy. This was at the same time as I was working on developing the Champions League, which had quickly become the world's largest and most prestigious tournament. Sometimes it felt like sport was more about money and my work more about politics than football. I had meetings with EU representatives and often spoke with Sweden's then Prime Minister, Göran Persson, to make it easier for footballers to work within Europe.

For the national team, the new millennium began with a new national team manager. An old AIK acquaintance, Tommy Söderberg, who coached AIK in 1991–1993, took over from Tommy Svensson, whose national team had missed both the European Championship in 1996 and the World Cup in 1998. Söderberg was a popular leader who, through his work with the national team's under 21 squad, followed many of the A team players on their journey to the national team. Many of the players who were dominant during the 90s now had to make way for new talents.

Sweden qualified for the European Championship, which was to be decided in Belgium and Holland during the summer of 2000. For the championship, Tommy Söderberg was joined by Lars Lagerbäck when it was decided that the national team would have two coaches for the first time. They couldn't be more different, but they were popular with the players, and the press dubbed the duo Lars-Tommy.

The championship itself was, however, one of the national team's biggest failures. Sweden was eliminated in the group stage. The media criticised Sweden's game and they talked about 'the boring national team.'

Sweden managed to score two goals, both from Celtic players. First it was AIK's golden hero from 1998, Johan Mjällby, who scored against Belgium, and then Henrik Larsson who scored against Italy. Sweden's 0–0 match against Turkey was named the most boring event of the tournament.

France won the second major tournament in a row, after beating Italy in a dramatic final where the French equalised in the last minutes. Trezeguet, in extra time, scored the golden goal, which was applied for the first time in a championship.

Despite the Swedish fiasco, there were certain players who stood out, which gave hope for the future. One of them was Henrik Larson. Although he was already in the 1994 World Cup, he was now a more rounded and complete player. After leaving Helsingborg for Feyenoord in Holland, where he didn't thrive, he was rightfully signed to Celtic in Scotland. The fans embraced him and he blossomed into one of Celtic's and the national team's leading players. The year after the Euro 2000, Henrik Larsson would win the Golden Boot as Europe's top scorer, and that was just the beginning of a fabulous career. A couple of years later, I would be able to hand him a trophy after the Champions League win with Barcelona in 2006, when he proved to everyone once and for all that he was of the very highest class. It is a very nice memory for me.

It was a new millennium and time to break up with the previous one. We discussed replacing the trophy that was awarded to the winner of the Swedish national league. The reason was that it had become known that Count Clarence von Rosen, who had given his name to the previous trophy, was a staunch Nazi sympathiser. It was decided that the new trophy would be named after someone who meant a lot to Swedish football. It was with enormous pride that I found out that the trophy would be called Lennart Johansson's trophy. Suddenly I became the little boy again, who wanted nothing more than for Dad to see my achievements.

The job of designing the trophy went to Anja Nibbler Kothe and as inspiration was chosen the trophy that Börje Leander, 'Garvis' and the other Swedish heroes held up in triumph at the Olympics in London in 1948. The production of the trophy itself was done by Ingemar Eklund, and since Hammarby was first team to hold up the new trophy when they won their only gold to date in 2001, rumours began to spread about secret inscriptions in the trophy.

Goldsmith Peter Gustafsson, who was a colleague of Ingemar Eklund, said in an interview that Ingemar had engraved 'Bajen forever' inside the ball that adorns the trophy. Most people thought it was a hoax until Ingemar's daughter confirmed the story.

It finally led to the Football Association deciding that a peephole operation would be carried out on the ball to see if there was any truth to the rumours. To everyone's surprise, there was a secret inscription in the ball, but it was not what Peter Gustafsson thought. It said 'Djurgården is the best' and the four names T Henriksson, Anna, Ludvig and Leopold. The chairman of the Swedish Football Association, Lars-Åke Lagrell, announced that the inscription would be removed immediately before the crowning of the next champion.

When Hammarby won the SM gold in 2001, they became the first to receive the Lennart Johansson Trophy. Djurgården took second place that year, while AIK had to settle for the 'little silver' - third place.

While Hammarby celebrated the SM gold, an airplane circled over the Sports Park in Sundsvall with a banner: 'Once is not enough.' It was a greeting from AIK supporters Christer Ericson and Tom Strand. It cost them 25,000 kroner to carry out the coup - but since then the two have invested considerably larger amounts to save AIK's finances.

25

Death's Group and Death's Grip

Actually, it was FIFA president Sepp Blatter's responsibility, but according to the rumour, João Havelange had told him that I was better suited for the task, and I had nothing against that. Therefore, in 2002 I was once again the person responsible for a World Cup, which this time took place in Japan/South Korea. The World Cup is the biggest sporting tournament in the world and I saw it as a great honour to be entrusted with leading the finals.

I thought it was really cool - and of course I shared the feeling with all the other Swedes - that Sweden had succeeded in qualifying for the World Cup. Unfortunately, both experts and other football lovers considered that we had been unlucky to be drawn into the 'group of death', as it was named, since the other three teams consisted of England, Argentina and Nigeria. Argentina was perhaps the biggest favourite to win the entire World Cup, and England – with Svennis as the national team manager – was another golden candidate. In addition, Nigeria had been one of the leading African teams for a few years and several of the players also played for big clubs in Europe.

England were favourites in the opener against Sweden despite not having won over the blue and yellow (the colours of the Swedish flag) in thirty-four years. That streak continued as the match ended 1-1. Meanwhile, Argentina beat Nigeria. In the next group stage match, England won surprisingly over Argentina, while Sweden beat Nigeria after two goals from Henrik Larsson. The match was a real nail biter before the last round.

Sweden's last group stage match was played in the morning Swedish time on 12th June, which coincided with the end of school that year. To avoid a conflict of interest, most schools chose to delay the closing by a couple of hours.

Sweden v Argentina became a Swedish football classic. The South Americans dominated, but it was the Swedes who took the lead with a dream goal by Anders Svensson through a fantastic free kick. Despite Argentina coming back and conceding a penalty, the match ended 1–1. Since no goals were scored between England and Nigeria, Sweden won the 'group of death' ahead of England, while the big favourite Argentina was eliminated. The same fate befell the reigning European and World Champions France, who were beaten in the first round of the group stage surprisingly by Senegal.

Now it was the Swedes' turn to meet the Senegalese, who were in their first World Cup tournament. The whole of Sweden was affected by football fever - again - and had it not been for the fact that a post stood in the way of Anders Svensson's shot against Senegal and that it was the last tournament to use the golden goal rule, the journey could have continued.

It ended when Senegal made it 2–1 in the attack after Svensson hit the post. It was a quick end after the impressive group game. Senegal then experienced the same thing when Turkey won on a golden goal in the quarter-finals.

Turkey also had its best championship ever and won the bronze medal after defeating host nation South Korea in the match for third prize.

In the final, football world giants Brazil and Germany battled it out over who were the best in the world. It was actually the first World Cup meeting between the nations.

It was the "Ronaldo Phenomenon" from Bento Ribeiro in Rio de Janeiro who, at the peak of his career, scored both goals in the final and took the trophy with him to Brazil.

During the World Cup, I handled the work without any major incidents. On the private level, however, life was still a little unstable. I partially got a new family when I met Lola, who had three children of her own. After a few years, when the worst time in connection with the divorce was over, I used to say in interviews that I had five children, which led to new conflicts.

My daughter Eva confronted me and said: "You have two children and if you want to name Lola's children you can call them bonus children or something else like everyone else does, otherwise I am going to end my relationship with you!"

I got angry with her and thought she couldn't say that to me, but Eva stood by her word, and to my great sadness we didn't meet for two years between 2003 and 2005.

It wasn't just on the family front that the situation was a bit turbulent. My health was not the best during this period. I had already suffered from prostate cancer in the late 90s, but it was diagnosed in time, so thank God it was curable. But my attitude to life has always been: 'As long as I'm smart, I'm going to stick with it.'

Unfortunately, your health is not something you can control and illnesses affect everyone whether you like it or not. For me, it meant that the cancer unfortunately found its way back to me, but this time, in 2005, I got cancer in the bowel. Fortunately, the doctors were also able to remove the tumour this time, even though the treatment took a lot out of me. But I have always thought that I have good genes - both my brothers lived to be over ninety years old and were in good health during almost their entire lives. To a certain extent, perhaps health also depends on how active and curious you are - body and soul often go together.

Despite the health problems and the fact that a few years earlier I had lost the election for the FIFA presidency against Sepp Blatter, I still wanted to be part of the football world both at home and in Europe. The fact that I was about to turn 75 was not something I wanted to let stop me. I am stubborn and wasn't ready to give up.

A tragic event touched me that year, 2003. We had lost away to Djurgården and then there was a national team break, I remember. That's when it happened. I got the same feeling as when Olof Palme was murdered in 1986, although perhaps this was even more surreal because it happened at the NK (Nordiska Kompaniet) department store, in the middle of Stockholm, in the middle of the day in front of hundreds of people. And perhaps it became even more unfathomable precisely because Sweden had already experienced the assassination of a prime minister. Something like that couldn't happen again, could it? It was with great sadness and dismay that I received the news of Anna Lindh's death. It felt like society had become tougher.

Side note: Anna Lindh was Sweden's minister for foreign affairs. On 10 September 2003 while shopping in the ladies' section of the Nordiska Kompaniet department store in central Stockholm for a televised debate later that night on the referendum about Sweden's adoption of the euro, Anna Lindh was stabbed in the chest, abdomen and arms. At the time, she was not protected by bodyguards from the Swedish Security Service; this proved controversial, given the similarity between Lindh's murder and that of Prime Minister Olof Palme in 1986 (the first murder of a government member in modern Swedish history).

26

Me and the Media

Now when I follow the media, I think how much worse it has become over time. The storms feel harsher and more merciless today. Over the years, it feels like the media carousel just spins faster and faster - with the internet, the media got a completely different competition to capture readers and viewers.

Even I have ended up in media storms and had to answer for things I said or did that could be misinterpreted or that were taken out of context. My worst crisis happened when I was secretly recorded at an airport. I was waiting for a flight home to Stockholm when a journalist I knew well came and sat down at the table where I was sitting. I, who never use a mobile phone myself, did not understand that he was recording what I said. In addition, there was no question of an interview but just a conversation between two people.

I told him that I had been to Cameroon, where I had participated in a meeting of the African Football Federation. Since for some reason I wanted to make it clear that I was the only European there, I said: "I entered a large room full of black people." A very bad choice of words. I should have thought about what I said but I really didn't mean anything by it.

A few days after our conversation, the journalist published an interview that was never an interview in the newspaper. After that I had to endure racist accusations, which made me very sad and angry. Few others from UEFA had then worked so hard to get a better cooperation with the African countries and to lift them up. Several of my closest friends in the world of football were from Africa. But when the merry-go-round starts, it's almost impossible to argue: the more you defend yourself, the more you feed the media monster. It went so far that I had to appear on a TV programme where Fredrik Belfrage (TV show host) asked questions about what had actually happened and whether there was any truth in what the journalist had written.

To emphasise that I have absolutely no racist views whatsoever, my friend Issa Hayatou contributed a link from Cameroon's capital, Yaoundé. As president of the African football federation, he believed that the Swedish people should be ashamed of accusing me of racism, as few Europeans have done more for African football than I have, according to Issa Hayatou.

Often during my career I have managed to solve problems before they were leaked to the media, where opinions and causes are quickly taken out of context.

I learned early on that it's good to be able to admit my own faults and shortcomings as frankly as you question others'. It's a question of credibility - nobody is perfect, but you should always strive to take responsibility and try to improve. Sometimes, however, it happens that you end up in difficulties with the press without even understanding why. You think you are saying something, but forget that if there is a will to make a false interpretation, then it is possible to for them to claim almost anything.

I went to watch when the Swedish women's national team qualified against England in Luton, just north of London. It was an autumn match and the pitch was a mud bath, but the Swedish girls fought bravely despite the poor conditions. Not only did they fight, they also managed to win. Afterwards I wanted to meet them so I went downstairs and waited outside the changing room.

When the players had showered and dressed, they came out one by one and I had the opportunity to greet everyone. Since a number of journalists were also waiting for the players, there were quite a lot of people in the corridor outside the changing room. I don't know to whom I said what I then said, but it was not meant in any negative way. Since the players had been covered in mud and dirt when they left the pitch, I hardly recognised them when they left the dressing room an hour later. They had put on make-up and ordinary clothes. That's what I happened to say.

Expressen's and SVT's (Swedish Television) journalist Pamela Andersson heard what I said and the next day she wrote an article to the effect that by commenting on the girls' appearance before and after the match I undermined their efforts. At first I didn't understand anything she wrote, but then I began to understand what she was after. That was absolutely not what I meant, although in retrospect perhaps I should have understood that it was easy to misinterpret if you wanted to. Despite the article, there was no harm done and I think that most people in football know how much work I do for the women's national team to have better conditions.

I am not perfect and such matters are inevitable if you are a public figure in today's media climate. But if there's one thing I'm proud of, it's that my intentions have never been murky. I've really tried to be fair. It is important not to take too much for granted and to trust one's values and that they lead the way.

27

Blatter Gets Booed and AIK in Crisis

The media pressure was great for our 'Superswedes' - Zlatan Ibrahimović, Henrik Larsson and Fredrik Ljungberg - to take us far. When Sweden beat Bulgaria 5–0 in the opening match of Euro 2004 in Portugal, the Swedes began to believe that something big was afoot. Our stars were in good form and all scored in the first match as well.

In the second round, against Italy, it looked bleak until Zlatan equalised with a magical goal in the final stages of the match. For the final round, Sweden, Denmark and Italy fought for two places in the quarter-finals. Sweden and Denmark could both advance if their match ended 2–2, which it did! Mattias Jonson's goal in the final minutes meant that the Italians missed out and they accused the Nordic teams of having settled the result in advance.

In the quarter-finals, the Swedish hopes of going far were also dashed as Holland won on penalties. The European Championship final was a 90-minute long match in which the home nation Portugal, led by new star Cristiano Ronaldo, struggled bloodily against Greece's compact defensive wall. Around 60,000 frustrated Portuguese chanted for their heroes in the stands, while the remaining 2,000 Greeks at the Estádio da Luz could not be heard.

But in the 57th minute, the arena fell silent when Angelos Charisteas made it 1-0 to the Greeks. Fear appeared in Cristiano Ronaldo's eyes. Although there were more than 30 minutes left, he and everyone else knew that Greece had not conceded any goals in the quarter- and semi-finals.

What should have been a national celebration instead became a painful and protracted battle against the clock and a Greek defence that looked like it could play for as long as it wanted. When the referee blew the final whistle, it was almost eerily quiet. Greece had won its first European Championship gold - one of the greatest football successes of all time at national team level.

I was there at the Estádio da Luz and remember it as an uneventful final, which gave rise to perhaps the biggest disappointment experienced in Lisbon. I sat and watched the final in the VIP seats and was applauded when I came on the big screen TV, but when they later showed Sepp Blatter, who was sitting next to me, the audience started booing. I pointed at the screen and said to Blatter: "Don't you hear that they are booing you?" but he just thought I was embarrassed for saying something so stupid.

After the final I went home to Stockholm where the Swedish league was soon to restart after a break, but I did so with an uneasy feeling in my stomach since AIK had started the season badly.

The team managed to pull themselves together during the season and saw that they had everything under control when there were three games left, but there was no room for error. By the time of the away match against Hammarby on 18th October, which was played at Råsunda for space and safety reasons, the Rats had to win in order not to end up in an even worse position.

When Hammarby scored 1-0 in the 67th minute, a few hundred members of the hard-pressed home crowd lost patience. They managed to kick up the gate to the north stand and some supporters entered the pitch. The match was interrupted for over 45 minutes before the police and security guards could sort out the disappointed supporters. AIK equalised but still failed to score a winning goal. Four days after the match, AIK's board announced the decision that the Rats would play the next home match without an audience, as punishment for the row in the previous match. The football association believed the punishment should be harsher than that, and announced that the club must pay 100,000 kroner in fines and any new qualifying matches would also be played without an audience.

The press wrote a lot about AIK's hooligans and the incident was the starting point for media coverage that AIK as a club is still alone in experiencing even today.

Råsunda new Stadium

On 24th October, the stands were gapingly empty at Råsunda. Apart from the necessary personnel, only Sanny Åslund, members of the board and others from AIK Fotboll AB's closest relatives are on site to see what would be AIK's last home match in the Allsvenskan for one and a half years.

Although I was welcome, I watched the end of the match from home and it was one of the saddest days I have had as an AIK supporter. It was for several different reasons that I chose not to go there. I was disconnected from the active work of the board because I was busy with my assignments at UEFA, but I also felt doubtful about the trends and opinions that were beginning to be heard both in and around the club. Because of the incorporation, people were drawn to the club for completely different reasons from me, and for the first time I began to have doubts.

The home stands in Råsunda gaped empty, at the same time as the journalists crowded the press seats to be there and write AIK's obituary. The players were almost paralysed by the strange atmosphere. After Örgryte's two quick goals at the end of the first half, the rest was just humiliation. When faithful Krister Nordin was sent off in the 47th minute, he symbolised an era that had passed. In total silence, he left the pitch. Örgryte managed to score 3–0 before the referee blew the final whistle, which felt like a liberation. The ones who were still eager for the match were the journalists, who competed to see who could give AIK the worst press.

It had been almost 70 years since I, as a small boy, saw my first match and although form has gone up and down many times over the years, the 2004 season was the worst so far. Nobody really knew what awaited AIK after that season, but I know that I both hoped and believed that we would come back straight away, because that's what we usually do.

At a press conference a few days after the end of the season, AIK announced that the board, coaches and CEO were resigning with immediate effect. My active career in the club included the fact that I left the position as chairman of AIK Fotboll AB to someone else.

At the same time, I sensed that a new era had begun and that there were elements that could also damage the club in the long term. I believe that although it is important to follow the global development of football, you must never lose contact with the grass roots, i.e. the club's members, who always stand up against the odds. They must support you and be behind you.

In the same way that our democracy is a fragile creation, a club's history, soul and self-image are also something worth protecting and preserving. When interests such as power and economics take over and dominate, it is easy for the club's foundation, i.e. the members, to become divided. It is often said that a society gets the politicians it deserves and perhaps it is the same in football, that a club management gets the supporters it deserves.

At the end of 2004, AIK was at a crossroads which, regardless of the choice, would pose major challenges. To win back one's status and the trust of the supporters, both hard work and great sacrifices were required.

There were obstacles on the way that it was impossible to get around. Sometimes you have to go straight through, even if it means that some things risk being lost forever. And even if AIK were to come back, a new era awaited. The storms that had previously often been weathered inside the boardroom would henceforth flare up in the media. There were power struggles between different phalanxes, who admittedly loved the same club but had different ideas about how it should be run.

The expected conflict was public, in the boardroom and in the stands. Football is passion and love, but sometimes the difference between love and hate is a thin thread that can break at any time.

28

A Message of Sorrow and a Last Attempt

It was immediately before the classic meeting against Öster in 2005 that I received the message that my former wife and mother to my daughters, Anna-Stina, had passed away. I was of course sad and bereaved, since Anna-Stina and I had lived a large part of our lives together. She was a wonderful mother to our daughters and I had great respect for her as a person and as a friend.

It wasn't just Anna-Stina who had been close to me, I became friends with her brother early on. He was AIK's and the national team's big star Börje Leander. Börje died two years before Anna-Stina, in 2003.

In a way, Anna-Stina's death thawed the frosty relationship I had with our daughters and our contact became better, something I am very happy about.

I understood that they wanted me to come to the funeral without Lola, which I did, both for their sake but also out of respect for Anna-Stina, who never really got over our divorce. Actually, I had hoped that she would meet someone new, but she remained single and that is something I am sad about. I wanted her to be happy and supported her throughout her life no matter what she wanted to do, but unfortunately she never found love again.

Anna-Stina's death was also a reminder of my own mortality - you never know how much time you have, and I had really always been on my way somewhere and rarely stopped. Many of my old friends had also already disappeared, and that obviously changed my social life as well.

Although 2005 was a year of sorrow, it still ended with great happiness when it was clear that AIK was back in the top league. I was convinced that it was important that we came back straight away because the finances would suffer if several years of Allsvenskan play were lost.

At the same time, at the age of seventy-six, I began to think about how long I could last and whether it was worth running for office again. I was faced with the decision that everyone with a long and successful career must eventually make, a decision whether to withdraw or continue. It is always easy in hindsight, but I felt that I wanted more and had more to give. Above all, there were many important battles to be fought. The world's biggest sport must be led by people who are honest and responsible, as FIFA's general secretary Jérôme Valcke had been suspended due to suspicions of ticket fraud. Now the rich European big clubs tried to push through a change that would mean that the confederations would be forced to pay big money to the clubs to get permission to play with the national team. It was to hit smaller associations hard.

In the long run, it was about inclusion and democracy. The reason why I hold association life so highly is that it builds from the bottom up and benefits everyone. And so I decided my work was not done yet and I needed to stand up for what I believed in again. Once I had made the decision to stand again for UEFA presidency, I realised that I would once again be pitted against an opponent who would use any means whatsoever to achieve his goal.

It had long been rumoured that Sepp Blatter would like to see the former great player Michel Platini as president of UEFA. The problem for Platini was that you had to sit on UEFA's executive committee in order to be elected, and France had already had another delegate there for a long time.

I still don't know how they went about firing this person to give Platini his place instead, but somehow they succeeded, and after that process Platini was available to run.

Considering how Blatter and his entourage managed their affairs internally, it was not the least bit surprising when Platini suddenly joined UEFA's executive committee. It was common knowledge that corruption and bribery were part of everyday life already when Havelange was president of FIFA, even if nothing could be proven.

What still makes me a little concerned and even sad is the way in which Blatter took advantage of my honesty. During a confidential meeting with him in 2006, he assured me that he wanted me to continue as UEFA president and that he intended to vote for me if I ran.

But when I read an article some time later, I realised that Sepp Blatter was once again playing tricks. In the article, Blatter said that Michel Platini was the one he should vote for as he had the qualities needed to take football into the future.

It was clear that Blatter bought votes and that the confidential conversation he had with me only a short time before had only been aimed at misleading me. The ulterior motive was probably to prevent Franz Beckenbauer from running for office; he was my friend and would never stand against me.

When the news of Blatter's support for Platini became known, my friend and colleague Lars-Christer Olsson announced that under no circumstances would he remain as general secretary of UEFA if I was not re-elected.

It was nice to feel his support. There is no doubt that Blatter was a shrewd businessman and even though I should have known better, he managed to trick me. That Platini was as false off the pitch as he had been brilliant on the pitch also became apparent. When I later confronted Blatter and asked why he first asked me to stay and then supported another candidate, he replied, "Such is life," and laughed.

Despite the bad odds, I therefore decided to run for office one last time. Whether it was a mistake is difficult to determine. With me at the helm, UEFA had grown and become an inclusive organisation, and I felt that the honesty and sense of justice I wanted to convey was still appreciated by many countries. Several members of UEFA's executive committee put their trust in me. Since there was no other candidate with my values and will, I felt that I had no choice but to stand up.

Everything I fought for was at stake because the opponents represented a view of football and power that went against what I wanted UEFA to be. So I maintained my candidacy.

I understood that it was going to be a dirty fight, but regardless of whether I lost it or not, I had to keep my head high. They shouldn't see any bad losers even though I felt sadness and hopelessness over the damage that Blatter and Platini could do to football. So I was going to make one more attempt; but first it was the World Cup, and there it was also going to be played behind the scenes...

29

A Match Within the Match

He used to be known as 'The Postman' or sometimes 'Bravo', but his real name was Stern John. In 2006 he played for Coventry City, but that was not where he celebrated his greatest triumphs. With seventy goals, he is Trinidad and Tobago's top scorer of all time.

Stern John

Together with West Ham's goalkeeper Shaka Hislop and Southampton's Kenwyne Jones, he made up the most famous players in the national team that faced Sweden in the opening match of the 2006 World Cup.

I was there for what was to become my last World Cup as organiser. At the same time as the game was going on below, another was going on in the stands. It was about trying to win support before the upcoming election; but it was difficult to compete against the cheats and tricks, and I would never go there. That was what it was all about. What remained was to talk to people and try to convince them that I was the best fit. I took the opportunity to speak with Franz Beckenbauer and other friends regarding the pending UEFA candidacy. In that sense, it was good that the World Cup was held in Germany. I have always had a good working relationship with the German association, even if we have not always agreed, and I count both Uli Hoeness and Franz Beckenbauer as close friends. The fact that it was Trinidad and Tobago that were Sweden's first opponents later became somewhat symbolic for me, as it would later become clear that the game on the field and the game in the stands were closely intertwined.

Everyone was convinced that Sweden with its 'Superswedes' would win over the small islands off the coast of Venezuela. Since Sweden had been drawn into a group with Paraguay and England, the match against Trinidad was of such a character that it had only to be won. But the seemingly easy task and the pressure made it more difficult and Sweden failed to score. It was a total failure and perhaps an ominous sign for me.

The day after the 0–0 match, bad press appeared in Sweden's daily newspapers about the national team's failure in the opener. It was clear that the team needed to get going against Paraguay in the next match. Sweden seemed to have as much difficulty scoring against Paraguay as against Trinidad and Tobago. But in the 89th minute – in what felt like Sweden's last chance – Johan Elmander hit a cross that found Marcus Allbäck at the far post. Allbäck had a bad angle and instead nicked the ball to an onrushing Fredrik Ljungberg, who via his forehead placed the ball into the right side of the goal.

The win against Paraguay meant that Sweden, like England, had qualified for the next round even before the last group stage match. This match was to decide which team won the group and thus missed the host nation Germany in the round of 16, one of the favourites to win the tournament. For England, a win also meant that a nearly forty-year-long curse could be broken. That's how long it had been since England last defeated Sweden in a competitive match. In that way, it was an extra exciting meeting. During the match I sat next to Bobby Charlton, who is a man I have great admiration for both as a player and as a person.

Bobby Charlton is one of England's most meritorious players and also one of the few Manchester United players who survived the tragic plane crash in Munich in 1958. Then Bobby was one of all the talented players who were part of the team that is still considered to be the best Manchester United ever created.

Immediately after the crash, Charlton decided to end his career. It was a decision that he later changed, and after his return he became one of the club's most successful players, with the World Cup win on home soil in 1966 as his crowning achievement.

As usual, it was an even and tough match when Sweden and England collided. The final result was 2–2, which meant that England won the group and wouldn't have to play the Germans in the next match, but bitter for the Englishmen was that the long streak of matches without a win against Sweden also remained intact.

If Sweden never used to lose against the English, the situation was the exact opposite when it came to the Germans. Shortly in to the match it was 0–2 to Germany, which also remained the final result. It was a disappointment of course, but the game goes on, both on and off the field. In the final, Italy faced France. France were the favourites.

In addition, everyone knew before the match that this was the last for one of history's greatest, Zinedine Zidane, who announced that he was going to hang up his boots immediately after the final.

The fact that France reached the final was naturally favourable for Platini's upcoming UEFA candidacy, even if the outcome was perhaps not the one he wanted. I sat in the VIP seats and even if it wasn't clear at the time, there was a nagging feeling that it could also be my last World Cup final as president of UEFA. It was one of the strangest and most remembered finals in World Cup history, for better or for worse.

On the one hand, one of football's greats crowned his career by scoring an impeccable penalty after just seven minutes: Zidane chipped the penalty over a surprised Gianluigi Buffon. The ball then hit the underside of the crossbar and landed just inside the goal line.

If Zinedine Zidane represented the beautiful game, he had his opposite in Italy's back line in the form of Inter defender Marco Materazzi: a hard, tough player who often played on the edge of what was permitted but who was also a dangerous attacking weapon in set pieces. Materazzi took advantage of the latter when he nodded in the goal after 20 minutes.

After the goal, the match became an even closer story and there was also friction between players from both teams. Materazzi, who had made a name for himself as one of football's biggest trash-talkers, stayed close to Zidane and talked eagerly with both referees and opposing players.

The match went to extra time. That's when it happened - why is still not entirely clear. On the pitch, Zidane is seen walking past Materazzi before turning around, taking a few steps forward and then headbutting the Italian in the chest with such force that he falls to the ground. For a brief second it felt as if time stood still. What happened? And why?

The referee had no choice but to show the red card and Zidane went with determined steps off the pitch. Before he went off, he stopped, ran back and took off the captain's armband, which he gave to one of his fellow players.

In the meantime, Materazzi had been helped to his feet by his teammates and could continue the match. That he said something very offensive to Zidane is obvious. Despite this, the continuation of the match and the subsequent penalty shoot-out were almost forgotten because Zidane, in his last match of his career, chose to headbutt Materazzi.

In the penalty shootout, Italy got its revenge on the French for the European Championship in 2000 and despite the fact that Italy was again the champion, it was a win with a bitter aftertaste. Afterwards, it was all about Zidane. The question all journalists were asking was what Materazzi said that made Zidane make the fateful decision.

Zidane, who always said yes when journalists wanted interviews, went out and apologised to all the children who watched the final for his behaviour, while he was clear that he did not want to apologise to Materazzi.

In retrospect, I can't get over the thought that, right then and there, it was another sign of what awaited me. Zidane against Materazzi had something of a good against evil feeling about it. Not because I'm someone who claims to be an angel, but I had I stood up against something that was bad. I hated corruption, and I saw how it ate up the sport.

Preparations for the election of the UEFA president were in full swing during the World Cup. According to several Swedish journalists, the French World Cup delegation was very accessible when the Swedish press was around. I also saw what was going on behind the scenes but chose to pretend it was nothing.

After the suspected corruption scandal in connection with Blatter winning the FIFA candidacy in 1998, many journalists began to scrutinise the affairs and decisions of both FIFA and the IOC (International Olympic Committee). But so far it was only suspicions and indications. Personally, I felt there was no doubt. One of the suspicions that abounded in the early 2000s was that Jack Warner, the soccer legend from Trinidad and Tobago, was involved in Blatter's candidacy.

As a member of FIFA's executive committee since 1983, Jack Warner had strong ties to both João Havelange and Sepp Blatter. Rumours swirled about backhanded money in return for support. The fact that he was already suspected of corruption in the 1980s strengthened the suspicions that he was involved in the 1998 election fraud.

During the World Cup there was nothing we could prove. Still. From there comes the bitter symbolism for me of Sweden's first opponent being Trinidad and Tobago, where Jack Warner was the highest authority. And of course, there were many of us who raised our eyebrows when it became clear that Trinidad and Tobago had qualified for the World Cup 2006. But again there is no evidence that it was cheating. After the 2006 World Cup, football in Europe faced a choice. Perhaps not everyone understood the importance of the upcoming UEFA elections, but it would not be long before they would notice the differences.

The election was held in January 2007 in Düsseldorf. While waiting for the result, the mood was tense. According to the information I had received about the number of votes for my name, I should win, but I knew what I was up against. At one point, Platini passed behind me and just as he passed, he put a hand on my shoulder. I sat and looked down at the table. This brief scene is immortalised by a photographer. It was as if we both actually knew the outcome. Just as in the 1998 election, the delegates faltered at the last minute. Once again, several people said one thing but then voted in a different way. Blatter's friend Platini got 27 votes and I got 23. Two votes were declared invalid. I had suspected this would happen, but I had to try.

"It's over now, I've done my part," I said to a journalist afterwards. My career came to an abrupt end when I left UEFA in 2007.

The first thing Michel Platini did was to appoint me honorary chairman. I got a standing ovation. I was honoured of course, but at the same time I felt the discomfort and frustration when I once again saw people who had just let me down now stand up and pay tribute to me. The corruption, the money and the fakery showed so clearly. Now I just wanted to go home.

30

The Long Road Out of Defeat

After the loss in the 2007 UEFA election, I withdrew from the international scene, but I was still active at home in Sweden with various assignments. It took me a long time to get over the loss, and for several months I had difficulty sleeping. I lay awake thinking about how it could have turned out the way it did. It felt humiliating.

Finally, I felt I had to clean up all the crap out of my system. I invited Sepp Blatter to Stockholm. It was a nice day. We met at Drottningholm's Inn. With me was Mija Lindberg, my long-time secretary and rock. Sepp Blatter also came with his secretary. The inn was empty of people; I had arranged that. Outside, the swallows flew high in the blue sky. Inside there was a heavy air. You could feel the atmosphere.

I wanted to know, hear it from him, why he had done what he did. But Blatter was slippery as an eel and in response to my questions it was either one thing and then another. I was boiling inside and finally couldn't keep it in. I raised my voice, almost screamed, something that for me is very unusual.

"Now I'm moving on. But you have to live with this for the rest of your life."

Just over a year later, also on a beautiful spring day, I was in the countryside and about to take a shower when everything suddenly went black. I fell and hit my head on the tiles. It was my youngest daughter Lena who took the call. Lola was shocked and did not immediately tell her how serious it was.

The emergency centre understood the seriousness and took me in a helicopter ambulance. The doctors quickly established that I had suffered a severe stroke, a stroke that was a hair's breadth away from costing me my life. When Lena then came to Norrtälje hospital, she first thought I had died. The paralysis in my face and one side of my body had deformed my face and I was barely conscious.

It was touch and go. The time after the stroke was frustrating. It was an incredibly tough rehabilitation and without Lola's support I wouldn't have been able to cope. Slowly, I began to regain feeling in my face and could begin to make myself understood. I became both restless and angry at having to spend so long in hospital. Throughout my life I have been used to fending for myself, and it was difficult to feel so weak. The fact that Lola underwent a major hip operation just before the summer made it even more difficult to look after me at home as we both needed support. Now a long way back to a somewhat normal life awaited.

I was lucky to survive, the doctors said, and I realised that I should be grateful that I got to hang on one more day. From the hospital bed, I followed what was happening in the world and how AIK was doing. I never fully recovered after my stroke and Lola had to help me with a lot of things.

The road back was long, and I thought a lot about my own mortality. I had stepped down from the international scene but still had a number of assignments back home in Sweden, and I was honorary chairman of UEFA.

My passion for sport and especially football burned as strong as ever, the glow in me had not been extinguished, the lust for revenge and frustration burned. Something had to be done. From IK Hjelm to UEFA, I had believed in the power of sport as a builder of positive values. Now I saw it being destroyed by greedy people. How do you combat that and how do you have a lasting effect? I often came back to such thoughts during these years.

It had been almost ten years since my stroke when my friend and lawyer Johan Strömberg called me one day and said he wanted to meet. Johan and I have worked together a lot, he had been chairman of AIK's main board and in AIK Fotboll AB and we had worked together in connection with AIK's and the national team's matches.

A few days after the conversation, we met outside at Vätö and it turned out that he had been thinking about the same issues as me, how to build values in the long term. Johan had sketched an idea to create a foundation in my name. A foundation that would work for the causes that I had worked for all these years. I thought it was a great idea, and even Lola, who heard us sitting and talking, came and told me that she thought it sounded like a very good idea.

Together we came up with what it should look like, what purpose it should have and, above all, which keywords should guide the foundation's operations. Johan, Jonas Mannerfeldt and I financed the start-up and Johan's colleague Klara Blomkvist took on the important role of secretary. The four of us became the board.

When the board was in place, we reached out with questions to people who could make up the foundation's advisory board. We got good names, such as the Portuguese football star Luís Figo, Per Strömberg, who is Johan's brother and chairman of the Nobel Foundation, and Jacob Dahlborg, who is the son of the former head of Nordbanken, Hans Dahlborg, a close friend of me and Lola. The foundation's aim is to promote the conditions for good leadership within the national and international football clubs with a focus on democracy, equality and anti-corruption.

We decided that the operation should be based on the following five points:

1. To organise high-quality training in sports management, with a focus on democracy, equality issues, knowledge for combating bribery and corruption, the football association's regulations as well as commercial issues

2. Offer scholarships for studies within the foundation's area of operation

3. Promote the development of international networks to increase knowledge of these issues in the various parts of the world

4. Issue publications related to the foundation's area of operation

5. To award the Lennart Johansson Award annually to recognise efforts in terms of good leadership in football

It should hopefully be a tool for change. It also felt extra good that Lola liked the idea so clearly from the start. Lola was my better half after all.

We received financial support from UEFA and the Swedish Football Association. And as part of our business, UEFA established a scholarship in my name. The scholarship recipients receive a contribution to the term fee for UEFA's manager training. The first board meeting where we awarded scholarships was in Lyon 2018, in conjunction with the Europa League final between Atlético Madrid and Marseille. It was a wonderful feeling to once again swing the chairman's baton at a meeting.

31

Life's Brutality and a Beautiful Victory

When the Christmas weekend, with all the visits and dinners, was over, it was just me and Lola in the apartment on 30 December 2017, the day before New Year's Eve.

Lola had been to the bathroom and cleaned herself up, putting on make up and fixing her hair. She had been to the hairdresser the same day and we were going home for dinner with one of the children in the evening. I sat in my armchair and Lola came out and sat in hers. On the purple glass table between us, we had each poured a drink. I remember that I thought she was very beautiful, as beautiful as when we first met.

We chatted a little about everything and nothing, as you do when you have been together for as long as we had been. Lola was happy that day, she was thinking about buying a new dress for the New Year. For almost forty years we had stayed together. I remember her looking at me and I saw that something was not right. Suddenly she fell forward onto the floor and lay motionless. I pressed the alarm button I've had around my wrist ever since I had my stroke. Several times I pressed that alarm button, but somehow I realised that it was too late. Lola was dead and I couldn't do anything. First came the shock; I refused to accept what had happened, it had happened so suddenly. Then came the tears and the incredible helplessness. A fear washed over me. What would happen now? Why did it happen to her, not me?

Lola's sudden passing was an incredibly hard blow for me. After the funeral and all the paperwork that follows when one's life partner passes away, I flew to Stockholm in the spring and settled in the summer house on Vätö.

I sat there on the island of Vätö and mourned for the whole of the first summer. Every night during our forty years together I had talked to her about how the day had been. I continued to do that even though she had passed away. I felt a great need for it. What really felt the most difficult was getting over everything that should have been said and done, yet had not. All the quarrels that you later regret. You want to get things said and make amends, but now there is no possibility of that. Life is brutal that way, time marches on and you can't stop it or go back.

Over time, I have noticed that it is difficult to admit that I am alone. Maybe it's because I'm not very good at being alone. But sitting and brooding over what you should have done without having the opportunity to do it becomes a kind of artificial existence and you are eventually forced to push yourself out of your grief.

On the same day that the hedge blossomed, I interrupted my grief process and went to see AIK play at home. In addition, it was the World Cup in the summer and Sweden was going to participate, which meant that I also planned to go to Russia to watch the final. After Lola's passing, I was more dependent than before on the people around me, such as Mats Lindberg, an old hockey player in AIK, and his former wife and my long-time secretary Mija Lindberg. Without those two, I don't know what I would have done. I count them as my closest relatives. Mats drove me here and there, to meetings and matches, and constantly supported me. Both Mats and Mija have always shown enormous loyalty.

Later that year I did an interview with *Aftonbladet* newspaper, who visited me at the office at the association, where I told them about the grief I felt after Lola's passing, but also that I had decided that this would be my last year as an active member of AIK. As it turned out, it was going to be the best farewell I could wish for.

The end of the season that year was extremely exciting. AIK had been in the lead with a maximum of eight points, but due to some unlucky matches, IFK Norrköping just managed to get ahead and keep the gold fight alive.

With three rounds remaining, AIK travelled to a freezing town called Östersund, without the suspended Sebastian Larsson. After only ten minutes, the team's midfielder, Adu, received a red card for dangerous play. A straight red card also meant that he, who had been an important cog in AIK's team, missed the last two matches of the season.

AIK, led by the ever-thinking coach Henok Goitom, once again showed strong morale and succeeded with one man down for almost the entire match, still winning 2–1. The win meant that AIK's season could be decided with a win at home at Friends Arena against Sundsvall in the next match.

Ticket sales hit the roof and after just a few days the number of tickets sold was approaching 50,000. The match would be historic in many ways. When the team entered the field, the north stand held up a picture that brought tears to my eyes. There was a large picture of the trophy that bears my name and next to it a picture of me holding a glass of whiskey. On TV, they then zoomed in on me in the VIP seats, in one of the three leather armchairs which are also marked with my name.

Everything was set for the gold party of the century - if only we could manage to win. Ball possession was constantly over seventy percent, the bar was hit four times, once on the underside, via the goalkeeper's neck, and outside, and both the outside and inside of the post were hit by AIK shots; but nothing went into the goal. I was pissed off when they didn't win it. That's how I react. I'm a bad loser when it comes to AIK. We just shouldn't have missed that chance.

I was certainly not alone in feeling the frustration spread and the doubts begin to grow.

Now there was only one match left. Away against Kalmar FF. AIK's supporters were awarded a relatively large portion of the tickets since Kalmar itself had nothing to play for.

The tickets ran out in an hour, so AIK supporters started calling Kalmar's season ticket holders and paying several thousand for them to sell their tickets for the last match. When a surprised woman called Kalmar's office and said that someone from Stockholm wanted to buy her season ticket for 10,000 kroner, Kalmar finally said stop.

There were still over 10,000 supporters who went down to see the final game of the Allsvenskan in 2018.

I flew down with an AIK delegation and the trophy was also on the flight. Dared I believe in fate?

If the Allsvanskan 2018 had been a film, it would certainly have won an Oscar in the best screenplay category, I thought. Before the match started, AIK announced that neither goalkeeper Oscar Linnér nor Sebastian Larsson could play due to injuries - with Adu and Kristoffer Olsson suspended on top of this, Rikard Norling had almost had to work magic to get a midfield together. But it turned out that AIK 2018 was not like other teams in the club's history. Already from the first match, there was a plan, and above all a kind of determination in the team that almost made the collective uncontrollable. The pressure had been intense all season. From the media, experts, their own supporters, but perhaps above all from the players themselves. Henok Goitom had been an excellent manger, driving his style that included everyone in the team.

It was therefore a different AIK that went out at the Guldfågeln Arena in Kalmar, which was bathed in black and yellow, making it appear as if AIK was the home team. In the stands were the suspended and injured Daniel Sundgren, Kofi Adu, Kristoffer Olsson and on the bench was Sebastian Larsson, who stepped down during the warm-up due to the pain-relieving injection he received which caused him to lose feeling in his leg.

When the match kicked off, a nerve-wracking experience began for all supporters.

AIK needed a draw but the match was quite close, even though AIK managed to create a few corners, which unfortunately were scoreless.

AIK finally made it 1–0 and thus put a cautious hand on the cup - a tentative excitement appeared among the spectators: it was within reach now. The time left in the match felt like an eternity. As the clock ticked on, an incredible atmosphere spread, just waiting to be unleashed. When the referee blew the whistle, thousands and thousands of AIK supporters stormed onto the field. Per Karlsson, who played fifteen seasons for the club, was stripped of almost everything by supporters who wanted souvenirs. I saw him walking past the journalists and TV cameras wearing only his underpants and felt a tear roll down my cheek. This was almost better than what I dared to hope for. But reality would surpass the dream - again.

On the way out to receive the trophy that bears my name, every player passed me as I sat by the entrance. First came Henok Goitom, who accepted the trophy and bent down to give me a hug. Then they came one after another and did the same.

Being able to hand out 'my' trophy to 'my' club was something I had longed for. It is a beautiful memory and was actually one of the happiest moments of my life.

On the plane home, the noise level inside the cabin was louder and happier than on any of my thousands of flights. There was singing and cheering. At Arlanda Stockholm airport, specially chartered buses were waiting to take everyone to the big banquet at Friends Arena. My day had been long and I felt that the joy I had inside me was best managed if I went home. Mats Lindberg drove me home and that night I fell asleep with an immense sense of happiness in my body.

Epilogue

The Dirty Game

"Only memories can weave history together and make it understandable," I said during my farewell speech to Råsunda in 2012. Now that the waters of Lake Mälaren are lapping back and forth outside the window as they always have, I think of all the people, meetings, wins and losses. When the last match was played at Råsunda in 2012, I was one of the few who had seen both the first and the last match at the old National Arena. I almost feel dizzy when I think about it. AIK lost the last match, played against the Italian team Napoli, and three days later there was an 'open house' for supporters who came there and took souvenirs in the form of tufts of grass, goal nets, chairs and everything they could get their hands on. It was an emotional moment. An era was over.

But the memories remain.

I am proud. Somewhere on the bookshelf is a book called *The Dirty Game*. I was right in the end. One of those who dug the deepest into all the rumours of corruption was the Scottish investigative journalist, Andrew Jennings. His book *The Dirty Game*, published in 2015, deals with the dirty dealings of both FIFA and the IOC and led to several of the top figures in the organisations being exposed and punished with long suspensions, including Sepp Blatter and Michel Platini.

The rumours that were circulating in the early 2000s would prove to be true. Jack Warner had been involved in Blatter's candidacy. Just as I thought. He had strong ties to both João Havelange and Sepp Blatter. The scandal unravelled and Jack Warner fell at the same time as Blatter and Platini, in 2015. It was proved that he had received a large sum of money before the 1998 FIFA election, when Blatter won over me. The money had been 'a gift' from João Havelange and, according to Jack Warner, was earmarked for building a sports facility in Trinidad.

Later, Jack Warner admitted that he had received six million dollars in a 'personal gift' from João Havelange to secure thirty votes for Sepp Blatter. The money was supposed to go to a training centre in Jack Warner's home country of Trinidad and Tobago, but he received it instead as a gift.

"Without our votes, Blatter would never have had a chance to be elected," Warner said three days after he himself resigned from his government post in Trinidad.

Money, corruption and greed galore. A huge scandal. It feels sad. But the truth always comes out in the end – and so it has this time too. It's a long road to winning back trust, I think. But the soul of sport cannot disappear, good will shall prevail. It always does.

A swallow flies acrobatically outside the window. I sit down in the armchair and put my hands in my lap. Proud but not satisfied, someone said.

Postscript

Lennart Johansson's Legacy

By Sören 'Sulo' Karlsson

Football, Rock 'n' Roll and the Fountain Of Youth

In Sweden, football is called the national sport. It may seem a bit strange in a country where the harsh winter sets the rules and forces us to conduct the competition season in spring/autumn instead of autumn/spring like the rest of the world. But there is something about football as a phenomenon that goes deep into people's souls, regardless of whether you were born in Gothenburg or Buenos Aires.

The sport has in many ways become a large part of human development. You learn to crawl, walk and talk and then run out to the other children in search of the ball that always seems to be rolling.

The street children in Brazil who kick a rag or a rolled-up newspaper, on the back streets of Birmingham with torn t-shirts as goalposts or on muddy fields in the Faroe Islands where the frost-bitten fields never let the grass grow. Football is the dream that in childhood makes us start to cooperate, see patterns and set goals.

It is the joy and freedom in symbiosis with what was later named "the beautiful game."

Anyone who wants to can join in and class differences, religion and social background are put aside when the game is on.

In many ways, football carries the same vision as the perfect society. A community for everyone, where the ball symbolises the globe that we must jointly take responsibility for.

The fact that elitism, money and career advancement then split the original ambitions is also reflected in society's constant struggle for success. A struggle that in the long run tears apart and divides in its pursuit of trophies and fame.

But if there was anything that was key to Lennart Johansson's view of the world's greatest sport, it was cohesion and equality.

Despite the huge salary accounts of the big clubs and the number of venture capital companies that wanted to own and refine them, he maintained his position. Some may think it is backward-looking, but nevertheless, it is and remains his legacy. A legacy as noble as it is honourable, and which the football world now has to manage.

Because when you sell passion, it is easy to forget where and how it was once born. Team affiliation, colours and lifelong love rarely begin in the FIFA corridors but instead have their origins on gravel pitches and grass patches where barefoot children fight over the shabby ball.

And Lennart Johansson never forgot the passion for the sport that gave him so much in life, despite his position at the top of world football. He constantly visited youth matches, training sessions for reserve teams and other activities that constitute football for most people. There, far away from Wembley, Nou Camp, royalty and dodgy dealings, he felt most at home.

Translating his view of football to today's professional activities is perhaps an impossible task. But it is good to periodically remind ourselves why football is so important to so many.

There are those who claim that a country's infrastructure and democracy can be read by watching its domestic football. And even if that is not entirely true, there is a lot in that statement. Injustice, class struggles and insecurity are easy to discern just by following football, and many war-torn countries try to continue the league game for as long as possible despite the bombs falling, as proof that the enemy at least cannot take that away from them.

During the intensive US bombing of Afghanistan in the wake of September 11th, it became big news when the football stadium in Kabul was razed to the ground. It was like a dagger into the heart of the nation and for that reason also a well-chosen target.

Football is in this way a symbol of hope. Pride and the dream of something greater.

I think Lennart Johansson understood this long before he entered the whirlwind of the football circus. He saw it when he looked at a bombed-out London as a 19-year-old, when Sweden won its Olympic gold medal, and he carried those impressions with him for the rest of his life. In this way, he becomes a rare representative of a sport which, no matter how you choose to look at it, is driven by the idea of winning.

But he knew that the people behind it, who make it possible, are just as important as those who shoot the ball into the goal.

Two years after his death, I took the initiative to create a foundation in Lennart Johansson's name. Together with his daughters and representatives from AIK, we established the Lennart Johansson scholarship, an award that will go to one of the many non-profit forces that a football club needs every year.

In this case, it will obviously go to his beloved AIK, which in many ways was his ticket to the world of football.

In this way, we also recognise the legacy of the country's greatest football leader. A leader whose heart and passion were always in the driver's seat and accompanied him throughout his career. A life's work that is unparalleled in Swedish sports history.

So who am I, then, who was given the honour of writing about his life, and what is my relationship with football?

Well, first of all, I am a die-hard AIK fan, just like Lennart, and I have also worked in various ways at the club. So when I was asked, it was obvious to say yes. But my interest in football started much earlier than that and, despite my long music career, has come to shape my life.

I was born into a football-mad family; both my father and older brother were active players and coaches high up in the league system. Next to the house where I grew up, there was a small grass field beside the railway where all summer days were spent together with the other kids in the area and where football was the main game.

Because it was a game. We pretended to be Beckenbauer, Cruijff, Keegan and others whose names we had learned by collecting football pictures.

That's probably where it started. Of course, then followed organised football at school and boys' team games, which some tired of while others continued. I belonged to the category that got tired, because I discovered the power of music in the form of punk, but my romantic approach to football always remained.

After having had the privilege of visiting more Allsvenskan stadiums than many of my peers during my childhood, I became a convinced AIK fan at the age of 5. Whether it was the impressive moves they brought to the away match against Norrköping or the stylish black shirts that made the decision, I will leave unsaid, but I had made my choice either way.

The fact that football and music were two very different things, and almost impossible to bring together in Sweden, did not bother me much. I continued to focus on music and kept my love of football as a complement in life. When bands like The Clash, Sex Pistols, etc. set the agenda for my listening, I also understood that both passions lived side by side in the England that influenced me so much during my teenage years.

Since then, football has always been there and given me experiences, drama and uncomplicated community when I needed it. I have largely retained the playful and, in some people's eyes, almost childish relationship with the sport. Because in the same way that music always keeps the heart young, football works in a similar way. As the legendary singer of Mott The Hoople, Ian Hunter, put it: "Sulo, if we keep playing rock 'n' roll we'll be teenagers forever."

I didn't doubt for a second that he was right.

Ian, who was a supporter of his hometown Northampton FC, was also living proof that passion for the club never ages. He told me that he still disliked George Best even though he had been dead for several years. The reason was an FA Cup match in the early 70s, when little Northampton was visited by the giants Manchester United. George Best had not played for a few weeks due to injury but was now back in the starting eleven. It was a historic battering at the then home stadium, The County Cricket Ground, when the home team fell 7-1 and George Best scored six goals. Since then, Ian Hunter disliked the Northern Irish slob who charmed the whole world and for a period was called the fifth Beatle.

With over 300 gigs in the UK, I can say that football and rock 'n' roll are in their DNA. Young, old, male or female, it doesn't matter. In the pub you socialise by talking about upcoming matches while the jukebox plays The Stones, Jam, Smiths, Oasis, Blur or The Kinks.

When I saw one of the best concerts of my life, Ray Davies from The Kinks in Stockholm, he opened the gig by stating that it was a good day today because Arsenal had just won 6-1.

My bandmate in The Crunch, Terry Chimes (The Clash), claimed every autumn that it was now West Ham's turn to win the league.

Another member of The Crunch, Mick Geggus (Cockney Rejects), is so associated with the aforementioned club that he played when the era of the Upton Park stadium went to hell.

During a short holiday in the Midlands, where my then eight-year-old son wanted to visit Sherwood Forest, we had lunch at a pub nearby. Two ladies in their 80s sitting at the table next to us asked if we were going to the game. We asked which game but realised it was a stupid question. It was of course about the nearby Lincoln match against visiting FC Barnet from London in the fourth division, called League Two. We had no intention of going but one of the ladies persuaded us and even let us park at her house so we avoided parking fines.

It was a wonderful experience in front of a sold-out stadium of about 5000 visitors, which ended with tea and cakes at the lady's house. Yet another proof that football is a door opener that builds bridges between both generations and nationalities.

Similarly, during my tours in the island kingdom I have seen Preston North End defeat Coventry, eaten an Indian takeaway directly from the pub inside Scunthorpe United's home stadium when they met Burton Albion, and witnessed my friends' beloved West Ham, etc., several times.

Sometimes, however, football can also be a marker of conflict. Before a gig in Glasgow together with The Damned, bassist Captain Sensible and I went to a Thai restaurant to pick up the catering. The food wasn't ready yet so we went into a nearby pub and ordered a pint each while waiting for our food to be delivered.

The woman behind the counter asked where I was from and I politely replied Sweden, whereupon the whole pub fell silent.

Since the average age of the clientele was high, we didn't really care, but when an old man came up and spat out a phrase in broad Glasgow dialect, I began to suspect something was wrong. When he then followed up the phrase by sticking out his tongue, I became really worried. Since I had difficulty understanding what he was saying, he repeated the procedure three times before I heard "Fucking Henrik Larsson."

After a quick look at the pictures that adorned the pub, where Paul Gascogne, Terry Venables and others hung among other icons from Glasgow Rangers' history, I understood why my Swedish origin had caused such a stir. Henrik Larsson was "Ghod and King Henric" on the other side of town where Celtic was worshipped and therefore more or less persona non grata on the blue and white side of Glasgow.

I said I wasn't interested in football and that's how I got out of trouble.

Another time I was dragged off stage in the middle of a gig at Witchwood in Manchester because I was wearing a red suit in front of an audience that clearly supported Manchester City. A mod who ignored my choice of clothes and wanted to hear the band took care of the problem and threw the person who had attacked me out.

On my honeymoon in Istanbul, there were no music or football activities on the schedule, but since "Europe's most dangerous derby" between Galatasaray and Fenerbahce was taking place during the time I was there, I managed not only to arrange tickets but also to convince my then-wife that it was an opportunity we absolutely could not miss.

The only problem was that it turned out that I had been given tickets for the Fenerbahce section of the stadium and that there was unrest among the 64,000 spectators, to say the least. The Turkish friend who had helped me get tickets also solved this problem by claiming that I was related to someone on the home team. The result was that we ended up in the VIP stands instead, for which I am eternally grateful.

Afterwards, it was important that I did not say that I was Swedish because Sven-Göran Eriksson was coaching the English national team at the time and a Turkish supporter had been stabbed to death by an English supporter a few months earlier.

The logic of football is not always crystal clear, but I managed without any scratches.

After twenty years of touring Spain, their football has also crossed my path in one way or another. A booker had a wife who worked at Real Madrid's headquarters, which meant that after a sold-out concert in the Spanish capital, he gifted me a gold-coloured ball with all the autographs from the star-studded team.

The fact that we then had a driver who liked rivals Atletico and therefore refused to drive past Real's home stadium even though it meant a detour just shows how strong an influence football has on our emotions and actions.

Of course, my most unforgettable memories are from the green field at AIK.

Nebosja Novakovic goals against AEK Athens and Barcelona, the gold in Gothenburg and most recently Sebastian Larsson's free kick in the gold hunt in 2018.

The latter because I was then finishing the Swedish version of this book and thought that Lennart Johansson's book really deserved to end with gold.

With his and my beloved AIK getting to lift the trophy that bears his name.

And so it was.

As if he had written the end of his story himself.

Sulo
Stockholm 2025

About the Author with Lennart Johansson
Sören 'Sulo' Karlsson

Sulo Karlsson has been carrying the torch for early 70s soulful rock 'n' roll well rooted in British history since the early 90s.

But besides his duty as lead singer in Diamond Dogs he is also something of a renaissance man.

Undoubtably one of Sweden's most prolific songwriters, through the years he has collaborated with many high profile artist such as Ian Hunter, Robert Wyatt, Janis Ian, Maria McKee, Crystal Gayle, Paul Young, Paul Brady and more.

His love of British music also led him to form The Crunch with former members of The Clash, Sham 69 & Cockney Rejects.

Sulo is also an author with six books released so far; and now he makes his debut in the UK, with the biography that he wrote together with the former UEFA president Lennart Johansson.

A book about a working class kid who had a dream that he fulfilled when he became one of the most powerful people in football history.

It's a stunning read about how he turned out to be the last honest man standing in a crooked football business filled with corruption and greed.

www.ingramcontent.com/pod-product-compliance
Lightning Source LLC
Chambersburg PA
CBHW070538170426

43200CB00011B/2464